# Washington Songs and Lore

# Washington Songs and Lore

Compiled by Linda Allen
Edited by Chrystle L. Snider,
Barbara Greene Chamberlain, and
John C. Shideler

Sponsored by the
1989 Washington Centennial Commission

## MELIOR PUBLICATIONS

Spokane, Washington

Cover design by Sandra Harner, Laing Communications Inc., Bellevue, Washington.
Book design by Sheryl Stewart, Melior Publications, Spokane, Washington.
Music typesetting by David Dutton, Spokane, Washington.
Typesetting by Spokane Imagesetting, Spokane, Washington.
Printing and binding by Publishers Press, Inc., Salt Lake City, Utah.

Compilation copyright © 1988 by the 1989 Washington Centennial Commission,
111 West Twenty-first Avenue, Olympia, Washington 98504.
Published by Melior Publications, P.O. Box 1905, Spokane, Washington 99210-1905.
All rights reserved, including the right of public performance.
Songs printed without a copyright notice are in the public domain
as defined under current U.S. copyright law and may be performed without permission.
Information enabling performers to contact copyright holders directly
for permission to perform is available from the publisher.
Printed in the United States of America.

**Library of Congress Cataloging in Publication Data**
Washington songs and lore.
"Sponsored by the 1989 Washington Centennial
Commission."
1. Folk music—Washington (State) 2. Music—
Washington (State) 3. Folk-songs, English—
Washington (State) 4. Songs, English—Washington
(State) I. Allen, Linda, 1945–    . II. Snider,
Chrystle L., 1962–
M1629.7.W3W37   1988               88-751873
ISBN 0-9616441-3-3

# Table of Contents

# Alphabetical List of Songs

# Foreword

This is a unique collection of music representing our state's musical heritage. Its creation was called for in a resolution adopted by our state legislature. And so the 1989 Washington Centennial Commission appointed a Songbook Committee to assemble songs old and new, serious and lighthearted, that were both significant and singable.

The Songbook Committee chose Bellingham songwriter and folksinger Linda Allen to compile this collection—which is unlike any other songbook that we have discovered—and to assemble historical information about the songs. The Songbook Committee met regularly for almost two years, listening to tapes, evaluating the list of titles—a labor of joy and good fellowship usually held at the home of Putnam Barber, the commission's executive secretary.

This is the distillation of that effort: the publication of a truly eclectic assortment of songs.

Many of the songs reflect the strongly held and divergent views that are characteristic of the citizens of our state.

The committee screened more than three hundred different songs to come up with this list of sixty-five which finally appear in print. We were not able to include every song that the committee chose, due to the unwillingness of copyright holders of some titles to allow their use.

In addition to this volume, we are pleased that the publisher has also undertaken to print an abridged version intended for school use.

The centennial of the state has been our motivation for producing this songbook. But an even stronger reason has brought this book into being: the joy of song that all of us can appreciate today and tomorrow. Our further hope is that it will give all of us a perspective on our own state which can be enjoyed no other way.

Wilfred R. Woods
Chairman, Songbook Committee
1989 Washington Centennial Commission

*"Folk songs are written, like all other songs, by individuals. All the folk have to do with them is to choose the ones that are to survive."*
—Henry Mencken

You are about to embark on a musical journey through over a hundred years of our state's history. Here you will find the songs which reflect Washington and its people, and songs which have been important in our history.

The songs were selected by a committee made up of teachers, folklorists, musicians, music educators, a newspaper publisher, a state representative, and the Centennial Commission's executive secretary. The result is a delightful mix of songs as diverse as the people whose lives and interests these songs represent.

My thanks to the Washington songmakers and the song collectors; the stage performers and the campfire singers; the dreamers and those inspired by their visions. Our state of Washington—its environment and its people—shaped these dreams and they are uniquely our own. Enjoy the journey!

*Linda Allen*
*Bellingham, 1987*

# Acknowledgements

Without the help and support of the people named here, and of so many others, this book would never have been born. Special thanks to Putnam Barber, Executive Secretary of the 1989 Washington Centennial Commission, for believing in this project. I'd also like to particularly thank Jens Lund of the Washington State Folklife Council for being a major contributor and supporter. Wilfred Woods, the Songbook Committee chairperson, kept us all on track with humor and grace. Also, thanks go to committee members Mark Dempsey and Barney McClure, who spent hour after hour playing through these songs, and Bob Cathey, of the Seattle Public Schools, who spent as many hours taping them for the committee. And in the final stages of compilation Scott Manawyddan provided an invaluable editing eye.

Also deserving of special mention are:

—The other members of the 1989 Washington Centennial Commission Songbook Committee: Sandy Bradley, Bruce Phillips, Rep. Dick Nelson, and Gina May of the Office of the Superintendent of Public Instruction.

—Howard Meyers, Jan Roberts, Phil Thomas, Mark Dempsey, and other collectors for being so generous with their recordings and songs.

—The staffs of the Seattle Public Library, the Washington State Library, the University of Washington Libraries, the Bellingham Public Library, the Tacoma Public Library, the Spokane Public Library, the Washington State University Library, and the Western Washington University Music Library, whose research proved so valuable.

—The staffs of the Bing Crosby Museum, the Whatcom Museum of History, the Museum of History and Industry in Seattle, the State Capital Museum in Olympia, the Washington State Archives in Olympia, the Washington State Museum in Tacoma, the Yakima Valley Museum, and other museums and historical institutions in our state who responded to our requests for historical material.

—Jean Gardner and Ralph Munro, Co-Chairs of the 1989 Washington Centennial Commission, for their support and continuing interest in this project.

—Dorothy Lindseth, Maura Craig, and the other staff members of the 1989 Washington Centennial Commission for keeping it all together.

—*Washington Magazine*, the *Seattle Post-Intelligencer*, the *Seattle Times*, the *Wenatchee World*, the *Tacoma News-Tribune*, the *Olympian*, *The Victory Folk and Jazz Review*, *Sing Out! Magazine*, Adelle Ferguson, Radio KUOW, Radio KGY, Radio KING, Radio KIRO, and the many other people, magazines, radio stations, and newspapers around our state who helped to get the word out.

—The staff at Melior Publications—John Shideler, Barbara Chamberlain, Chrystle Snider, and Sheryl Stewart—who all worked so hard to make this book a reality.

—Melior Publications would like to extend extra thanks to David Dutton, who worked wonders typesetting music that came in a *wide* variety of formats; to Barbara Porter, Bob Cathey, and Barney McClure for all their help proofreading the music; and to Al Richardson for his help with the copyright agreements.

—And of course, we *all* thank the hundreds of Washingtonians and former Washingtonians who wrote us to suggest a song or share a memory. Thank you all!

# My Native Land

*The Makah had all kinds of songs—love songs and fire songs that some people composed. They would have gatherings of just women sometimes, and I'd hear my grandmother singing her songs. Just the men would go to the bone games long ago. Long ago you couldn't do anything out of the way—someone would make a song out of it.*

*—Helen Peterson*
  *In an interview with Kathryn Bruneau*
  *Washington Women's Heritage*
    *Project*

*There were eight altogether in our family, and my mother was a very busy woman. . . . At night my dad played the fiddle, and he'd play little French songs and sing to us, and the family would sit around the stove in the parlor. We'd enjoy it so. And then he'd help mother with the little ones, getting them dressed and into bed.*

*—Josephine Thomas Amsel and Mabel*
    *Thomas Jones*
  *In an interview with Lorraine*
    *McConaghy*
  *Renton Historical Museum*

The history of our state is rich in musical traditions that go back centuries—from the ancient songs of our state's first people to modern interpretations of historical events. This chapter's examples of our cultural heritage help us to learn about our history through the songs of our people.

Johnny Moses is a traditional singer and spiritual leader of Salish and Nootka heritage who has kept alive the rich and precious tradition of native songs. **"Welcome Song"** and **"The Traveling Canoe Song,"** sung by Johnny Moses and transcribed by Dr. Loren Olsen of Washington State University, are both of Samish origin. " Welcome Song" comes from Samish Island and was sung on the beach as visitors arrived. "The Traveling Canoe Song," which comes from the Bow Hill area, describes the movement of paddles in the water, and is also used as a healing song.

The earliest known song not of native origin was "On The Discoveries Of Captain Lewis," a parody sung to the tune of "Yankee Doodle Dandy" that was written as a rebuttal to a poem composed for a testimonial dinner honoring the explorers Lewis and Clark. Written by Democratic poet and statesman Joel Barlow, the testimonial poem lavishly praised Thomas Jefferson, who sent the explorers on their journey in response to the competitive threat

*A native Washingtonian, here seen in "The Middle Columbia" by Edward Curtis. Courtesy of Washington State Historical Society.*

*Nez Perce natives.
Courtesy of Eastern
Washington State
Historical Society.*

from British and Canadian fur companies that
were profiting from the abundance of furs
available from Northwest Indian tribes. The
parody, rumored to have been written by John
Quincy Adams, criticizes the explorers for not
finding the lost tribe of "Welchman Indians,
mammoths, or the 'hog with a navel on its
back.'"

> "Good people, listen to my tale,
> 'Tis nothing but what true is;
> I'll tell you of the mighty deed
> Atchiev'd by Captain Lewis—
> How starting from the Atlantick shore
> By fair and easy motion,
> he journied, all the way by land,
> Until he met the ocean.
>
> Heroick, sure, the toil must be
> To travel through the woods, sir;
> And never met a foe yet save
> His person and his goods, sir!
> What marvels on the way he found
> He'll tell you, if inclin'd, sir—
> But I shall only now disclose the things he
>   did not find, sir."
> —*Music for Patriots, Politicians, and
>      Presidents
>    By Vera Brodsky Lawrence*

The Appaloosa horse has become a symbol
of the history of the Nez Perce people. **"The
Heart Of The Appaloosa"** tells the story of the
Nez Perce flight to avoid being forced onto a
reservation. In June 1877 Chief Joseph, the
leader of the Nez Perce tribe, was told that his
people had to move from their homeland in
Oregon's Wallowa Valley to a reservation in
Idaho. Although Joseph's forces won several of
the battles they fought, they soon realized that
they could not defeat the U.S. Army. The Nez
Perce began a retreat to Canada, where they
hoped to join forces with the Sioux. After
leading his tribe of women, children, and old
men more than fifteen hundred miles, Joseph
surrendered only thirty miles from the Canadian
border. He was later sent to the Colville
Reservation, where he died in 1904. It has been
said that the Appaloosa, bred and highly prized
by the Nez Perce, were killed by soldiers as a
way of stopping the Nez Perce flight. Although
there is disagreement among historians on this
point, it is clear that the Appaloosa continues in
folklore as, according to the song's composer
Fred Small, "an allegory of resurrection, of
rebirth, of continued struggle after apparent
annihilation."

The song most associated with pioneer settlement in Washington, **"Missionary's Farewell,"** was written by the Reverend Samuel F. Smith, the composer of "America." It was sung by Narcissa Whitman at her wedding in 1836. The next day Narcissa left her Angelica, New York, home with her new husband Marcus for Oregon Country, where the Whitmans established a mission among the Cayuse Indians in the Walla Walla Valley.

The Pig War of 1859 inspired several songs by modern songwriters. The 1978 song **" San Juan Pig"** tells the story fairly accurately. In June of 1859 an American settler named Lyman Cutler shot a pig belonging to the Canadian Hudson's Bay Company. The incident rapidly escalated, since the pig was shot on San Juan Island, disputed territory claimed by both Britain and the United States. Soldiers and warships descended on the area, with hotheads on both sides calling for war. Diplomacy and common sense eventually prevailed, and the boundary was settled through mediation by the German Kaiser in 1872.

**"Quincyland, My Quincyland,"** another parody of "Beulah Land" written by an unknown Quincy author, was first heard at the National Irrigation Congress in 1909. Quincy's enthusiastic delegation paraded the streets of Spokane carrying a banner and singing their booster song.

**"The Old Settler"** is the Northwest's most enduring folk song. Written around 1874 by police court judge Francis Henry and sung to the tune of "Old Rosin, The Beau," it appeared in Olympia's newspaper, the *Washington Standard,* in April 1877. Pete Seeger recently wrote that his "claim to fame" was that "it was me and Woody (Guthrie) that taught Ivar that song." And it was Ivar Haglund, a Seattle balladeer, who used the song extensively on his radio show during the 1940s. Haglund later named his restaurant from the last line of the ballad. A sequel to the tune appears in the introduction to chapter nine.

The hymns that promised a better life to come—the pioneer's dream—were favorites of the settlers. One of the most popular was "Beulah Land." The old hymn was utilized as the basis for a number of parodies like this one:

> I've reached the land of rain and mud
> Where flowers and trees so early bud
> Where it rains and rains both night and day
> For in Oregon, it rains always.
>
> Oregon, wet Oregon
> As through thy rain and mud I run
> I stand and look out all around,
> And watch the rain soak in the ground.
> Look up and see the waters pour,
> And wish it wouldn't rain no more.
> —*From the collection of Barre Toelken*

Fifty years after the original the tune was used for a song by Horace Taylor entitled "Washington: A Geography Lesson On Puget Sound in 1890." His first verse is as follows:

> I've reached the land of fish and clams
> And spuds and cabbages and fine hams
> Here weep all night the low'ring clouds
> And earth is dressed in greenest shrouds.
> —*From the collection of Dick Fallis*
> *Historian, Skagit County Pioneer*
> *Association*

Historical events are preserved in many ways: newspaper accounts, journals and letters, and the memories of those within the community. Yet as the books and newspapers fade, and survivors of an event pass away, the impact is lost. In songs we find some of the truest expressions of how ordinary people viewed their experiences and of how they felt about their lives.

# Welcome Song

As sung by Johnny Moses
Transcribed by Dr. Loren Olsen

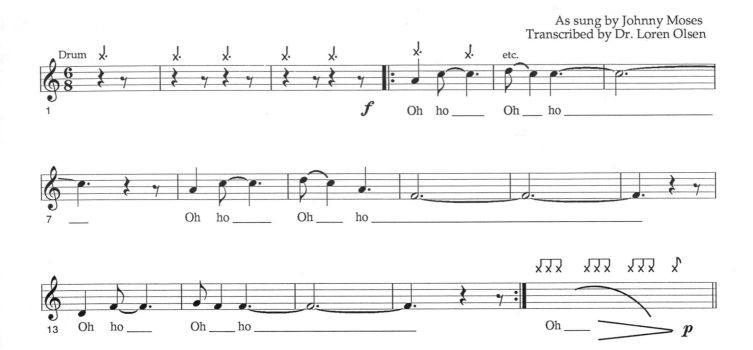

4

# The Traveling Canoe Song

As sung by Johnny Moses
Transcribed by Dr. Loren Olsen

5

# The Heart Of The Appaloosa

Words and music by Fred Small

**5.** The chief spoke to the People in his anger and his pain,
"I am no more Chief Joseph. Rolling Thunder is my name.
They condemn us to a wasteland of barren soil and stone.
We shall fight them if we must, but we will find another home."

6.    They fled into the Bitterroot, an army at their
heels.
They fought at White Bird Canyon, they fought at
Misery Hill.
Till the colonel saw his strategy and sent the order
down:
Kill the Appaloosa wherever it be found.

*CHORUS*

7.    Twelve hundred miles retreating, three times over
the Divide,
The horse their only safety, their only ally.
Three thousand Appaloosas perished with the
tribe,
The people and the horses dying side by side.

8.    Thunder Rolling in the Mountains said, "My heart
is sick and sad.
Our children now are freezing. The old chiefs are
dead.
The hunger takes our spirit. Our wounds are deep
and sore.
From where the sun now stands I shall fight no
more."

*CHORUS*

9.    They were sent to Oklahoma, malaria ran rife,
But more died of broken hearts far from the land
that gave them life.
And the man once called Joseph at death was
heard to say,
"We have given up our horses. They have gone
away."

10.    But sometimes without warning from a dull
domestic herd
A spotted horse of spirit wondrous will emerge.
Strong it is and fearless and nimble on a hill,
Listening for thunder, the Appaloosa's living still.

*CHORUS*

SNOHOMISH "CHIEF SHELTON"

*Drawing of Snohomish "Chief Shelton" by Robert Aiston.*
*Courtesy of Rich and Lylene Johnson.*

# Missionary's Farewell

Words by Rev. Samuel F. Smith
Tune : Traditional

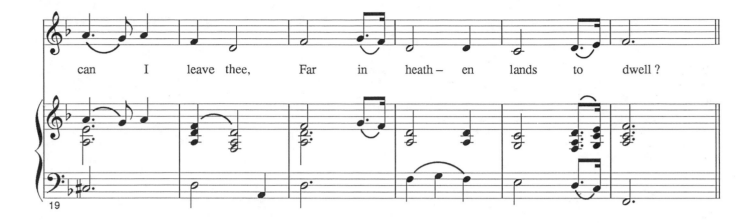

can      I      leave thee,    Far    in    heath — en    lands    to    dwell ?

---

2.    Home!—thy joys are passing lovely—
       Joys no stranger-heart can tell;
       Happy home!—'tis sure I love thee!
       Can I—can I say—Farewell?

       *CHORUS*

3.    Yes! I hasten gladly,
       From the scenes I love so well;
       Far away, ye billows bear me;
       Lovely native land!—farewell!

       *SECOND CHORUS*
       *Pleased I leave thee, pleased I leave thee,*
       *Far in heathen lands to dwell.*
       *Pleased I leave thee, pleased I leave thee,*
       *Far in heathen lands to dwell.*

4.    In the deserts let me labor,
       On the mountains let me tell,
       How he died—the blessed Saviour
       To redeem a world from hell!

       *THIRD CHORUS*
       *Let me hasten, let me hasten,*
       *Far in heathen lands to dwell.*
       *Let me hasten, let me hasten,*
       *Far in heathen lands to dwell.*

# San Juan Pig

Words and music by
John Dwyer

3.  When he saw the pig a-rootin', Lyman Cutler, he
        got sore.
    He grabbed up his musket, for the pig he tore.
    The pig saw him comin' and headed for the
        woods,
    But he stopped at the edge, and Cutler shot him
        good.

4.  Then Cutler felt regretful and went down to
        Hudson's Bay,
    And told the clerk in charge of the porker he
        would pay.
    Griffin said, "One hundred dollars, he's a prize
        breeding boar."
    Cutler told him "I'll pay three, and not a penny
        more."

5.    Then up stepped A. G. Dallas, and said, "See here,
           my man,
    You're already trespassing upon Canadian land.
    You know it's British country from Rosario to the
           west,"
    "Not so," said Lyman Cutler, "East of Haro is U. S."

6.    Well, the settlers they backed Cutler with their
           muskets in their hands.
    The British thought it wiser not to make a stand.
    The stars and stripes were hoisted to celebrate the
           day,
    And were seen by General Harney a-sailin' on the
           bay.

7.    The general came ashore and he listened to their
           tale.
    He was a man of action and to help he did not fail.
    To Fort Bellingham he sent 'ere he sailed away
           again,
    And down came Captain Pickett with a company
           of men.

8.    Then up sailed the British with war ships one,
           two, three,
    Which made a few too many for Pickett's
           company.
    They had to find a way to even up the score,
    So he sent to Fort Steilacoom and got five
           hundred more.

9.    Well they argued in the Senate, and in the House
           of Lords,
    And they didn't make much progress but they
           used a lot of words.
    So they asked the German Emperor the boundary
           to define,
    And tell those treaty makers where to draw the
           line.

10.    Now the Kaiser gave his answer in 1872,
    And said that Haro Strait was where the line went
           through.
    Well they called it a war, but it wasn't very big—
    And the only one got killed was a little British pig.

# Quincyland, My Quincyland

Author unknown
Tune : "Beulah Land"

1. You've reached the land of drought and heat Where no–thing grows for man to eat; The
2. Our hor—ses are of bron—co race Star—va–tion shows u—pon their face; We

wind that blows the bur–ning heat Brings no–thing for our stock to eat.
do not live, we on–ly stay We are too poor to get a–way.

**Chorus**

O Quin–cy–land, my Quin–cy–land ! As on this bur–ning soil we stand,

Then look a–way a—cross the plains And won–der why it ne–ver rains

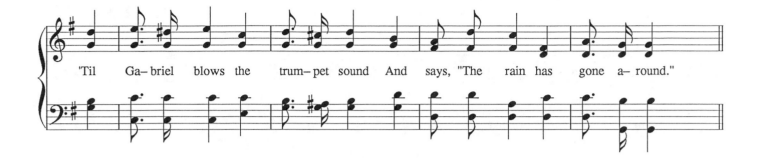

'Til Ga—briel blows the trum—pet sound And says, "The rain has gone a— round."

3.    We have no wheat, we have no oats
We have no corn to feed our shoats;
We have not much ourselves to eat
Our pigs are squealing around our feet.

*CHORUS*

4.    We've got soil and altitude,
We've got the sun to grow the food;
We've got the space and everything
'Cept water we ask Congress to bring.

*CHORUS*

5.    Now we hope your delegation
Favors Columbia Irrigation;
With water we will have prosperity
Come to this land of aridity.

# The Old Settler

Words by Francis Henry, 1874
Tune : Traditional

1. I'd trav—eled all o—ver the coun—try, Pros—pect—ing and dig—ging for gold, I'd tun—neled, hy—draul—icked and cra—dled, And I had been fre—quent—ly sold, And I had been fre—quent—ly sold, And I had been fre—quent—ly sold, I'd tun—neled, hy—draul—icked and cra—dled, And I had been fre—quent—ly sold.

2. Where one had made rich—es by mi—ning, Per—ceiv—ing that hun—dreds grew poor, I made up my mind to try farm—ing, The on—ly pur—suit that is sure, The on—ly pur—suit that is sure, The on—ly pur—suit that is sure, I made up my mind to try farm—ing, The on—ly pur—suit that is sure.

3. So, rolling my grub in my blankets,
   I left all my tools on the ground
   And started one morning to shank it,
   For a country they call Puget Sound.

   For a country they call Puget Sound,
   For a country they call Puget Sound,
   And started one morning to shank it,
   For a country they call Puget Sound.

4.   Arriving flat broke in mid-winter,
     I found it enveloped in fog,
     And covered all over with timber,
     As thick as the hair on a dog.
     As thick as the hair on a dog,
     As thick as the hair on a dog,
     And covered all over with timber,
     As thick as the hair on a dog.

5.   As I looked at the prospect so gloomy,
     The tears trickled over my face;
     For I felt that my travels had brought me,
     To the edge of the jumping-off place.
     To the edge of the jumping-off place,
     To the edge of the jumping-off place,
     For I felt that my travels had brought me
     To the edge of the jumping-off place.

6.   I took up a claim in the forest,
     And sat myself down hard to toil,
     For two years I chopped and I labored,
     But I never got down to the soil.
     But I never got down to the soil,
     But I never got down to the soil,
     For two years I chopped and I labored,
     But I never got down to the soil.

7.   I tried to get out of the country,
     But poverty forced me to stay,
     Until I became an old settler,
     Then nothing could drive me away.
     Then nothing could drive me away,
     Then nothing could drive me away,
     Until I became an old settler,
     Then nothing could drive me away.

8.   And now that I'm used to the climate,
     I think that if man ever found,
     A spot to live easy and happy,
     That Eden is on Puget Sound.
     That Eden is on Puget Sound,
     That Eden is on Puget Sound,
     A spot to live easy and happy,
     That Eden is on Puget Sound.

9.   No longer the slave of ambition,
     I laugh at the world and its shams,
     As I think of my pleasant condition,
     Surrounded by acres of clams.
     Surrounded by acres of clams,
     Surrounded by acres of clams,
     As I think of my pleasant condition,
     Surrounded by acres of clams.

# The Union's Inspiration

*These are struggle songs of the people. They are outbursts of bitterness, of hatred for the oppressor, of determination to endure hardships together and to fight for a better life. Whether they are ballads composed and sung by an individual, or rousing songs improvised on the picket line, they are imbued with the feeling of communality or togetherness. They are songs of unity, and therefore, most are songs of the union.*

—John Greenway
*American Folk Songs of Protest*

*Home musicale, 1896. Courtesy of John Schroeder Collection.*

The songs included in this chapter have sprung from the heart of the Northwest labor movement. It was in Spokane during 1906 that the struggling organization known as the Industrial Workers of the World (the Wobblies) was approached by a professional orator named Jack Walsh, who offered his services to literally "drum up" new members from the ranks of the unemployed. Walsh was initially drowned out by the bands of the Salvation Army and the Volunteers of America, so he organized his own band, with "Haywire Mac" McClintock on horn and a giant lumberjack on bass drum. Walsh added parodies of Salvation Army hymns to the repertoire, which had relied heavily on Mac's songs ("Big Rock Candy Mountain" and "Hallelujah, I'm A Bum," among others).

To grab the crowd's attention, the band hid in a doorway while one member, dressed in a bowler hat and carrying a briefcase and umbrella, yelled to the crowd, "Help! I've been robbed!" The crowd rushed over only to hear, "I've been robbed by the capitalist system!

Fellow workers. . . ." He then launched into a short speech, and the makeshift band stepped out of the doorway and played their songs. Four of the band's songs were made into a ten cent leaflet that grew into the famous *Little Red Songbook,* the Wobbly "bible." Street singing and organizing became the principal activities of the Northwest Wobblies.

Joe Hill, a Swedish-American migrant worker who wrote songs for the Wobblies, wrote a special version of a favorite Salvation Army hymn for the IWW. **"The Preacher And The Slave"** is sung to the tune of "The Sweet Bye And Bye" and is alleged to have been written to gain support for the Wobblies' Free Speech Fight. The Free Speech Fight arose in response to a hastily passed Spokane ordinance that banned public speaking downtown—an ordinance pushed through by the "job sellers" who were under attack by the IWW. But the Wobblies exercised their First Amendment right to free speech and disobeyed the ordinance. Wobbly leaders encouraged their members to give soapbox speeches all over town. When one Wobbly was arrested and carried off to jail, ten more lined up to take his place. Soon hundreds of Wobblies had been arrested, the jails were filled, and the city council was forced to change the law. This gave the Wobblies their first national exposure.

In 1915 Ralph Chaplin wrote what became the theme song of the American labor movement—**"Solidarity Forever."** In an article published in 1960 Chaplin wrote:

> *Even at this late hour, I am more grimly convinced than ever that neither the song itself nor the organization that sparked it could have emerged from any environment other than the Pacific Northwest in the afterglow of the rugged period of American pioneering . . . . It is true that 'Solidarity Forever' was written in Chicago, but it is also true that nobody ever heard of it until fifty thousand striking Puget Sound loggers bellered it out to a world that didn't care a hoot about the problems of voteless and cruelly exploited 'timber beasts' . . . that it became the theme song of the 'fighting, singing I.W.W.' is understandable; that it became, at a later date, the theme song of the not-so-needy, not-so-worthy, so called 'industrial unions' spawned by an era of compulsory unionism is not so understandable.*

Some Wobblies lost their lives because of their beliefs. **"The Sentry,"** written in 1978, tells of an incident that occurred between American Legionnaires and the Wobblies in Centralia, where an atmosphere of suspicion and hatred existed between the lumber interests and the Wobblies.

A raid on the Wobbly hall was planned by the American Legion for Armistice Day, November 11, 1919 (today known as Veteran's Day). As the Legionnaires paraded in front of the Wobbly hall, they broke ranks and charged the building. Four Legionnaires died in the conflict. One Wobbly, Wesley Everest, fled. Everest was captured, tortured, and later hanged.

None of those participating in the lynching were ever brought to trial, but in a Montesano courtroom eight Wobblies—Britt Smith, O. C. Bland, Ray Becker, John Lamb, Bert Bland, Eugene Barnett, James McInerney, and Loren Roberts—were given maximum prison sentences for killing the Legionnaires. A bronze statue in a Centralia city park, dedicated to the Legionnaires who died, inspired this song.

**"Fifty Thousand Lumberjacks"** grew out of the 1917 lumber workers' strike in the Northwest. Organized by the Wobblies, loggers protested conditions in the camps—conditions that included rotting, filthy mattresses, roofless bunkhouses, no showers, no laundries or drying rooms, and substandard food. Loggers were

*Northwest loggers. Courtesy of Special Collections Division, University of Washington Libraries.*

*Near Grand Coulee Dam, 1938. Works Progress Administration photograph courtesy of Library of Congress.*

forced to carry their "bindles," or bedding, on their backs into the lumber camps, earning them the name "bindle stiffs." On May Day 1918, International Labor Day, lumber workers burned their bindles in protest for better working conditions. Wobbly organizers later called off the lumber workers' strike, but the Spruce Production Division, created by the U.S. government to produce timber needed for wartime aircraft production, almost immediately implemented the reforms for which the strikers had fought.

Laura Law was a woman deeply committed to the labor movement. In 1935 she helped maintain a soup kitchen which served three to four thousand men. She regularly appeared on picket lines. In 1936 she joined and became an officer of the ladies' auxiliary of the International Woodworkers of America. She believed that if conditions were to improve and wages increase, women had to become an integral part of the trade union movement. Beginning in late 1937 Laura and her husband, Dick, were the recipients of numerous phone calls and letters threatening them with violence if they didn't leave town.

**"Ballad Of Laura Law"** tells Laura's story. She was found brutally murdered in her home in Aberdeen on the evening of January 5, 1940. During the sensational coroner's inquest that followed, county prosecutors and the

attorneys for her parents and her husband all tried to develop a theory for the murder. Prosecutors questioned the whereabouts of Dick Law, his alleged affair with another woman, and his alleged involvement with Communism. Questions from the family's attorney centered on the labor movement activities of Dick and Laura, threats made against them, and the alleged reign of lawlessness in Grays Harbor County, aimed at the destruction of lumber industry unions, that may have led to the murder of Laura Law. The murderer of Laura Law was never identified.

> *Those that are responsible for the murder of my wife are the forces that have been endeavoring to destroy the labor movement, democracy, and civil liberties, and are particularly rampant right here in Aberdeen and on the Pacific Coast. . . . The bombing of several places here, the wrecking of the workers' halls, and the murder of my wife can't be separated.*
>
> *—Dick Law*

The songs of the Northwest labor movement are as bold and brassy as the movement itself. Although working conditions are safer, cleaner, and more humane, new songs reflecting our current struggles and dreams continue to be created.

# The Preacher And The Slave

Words by Joe Hill
Tune: "The Sweet Bye And Bye"

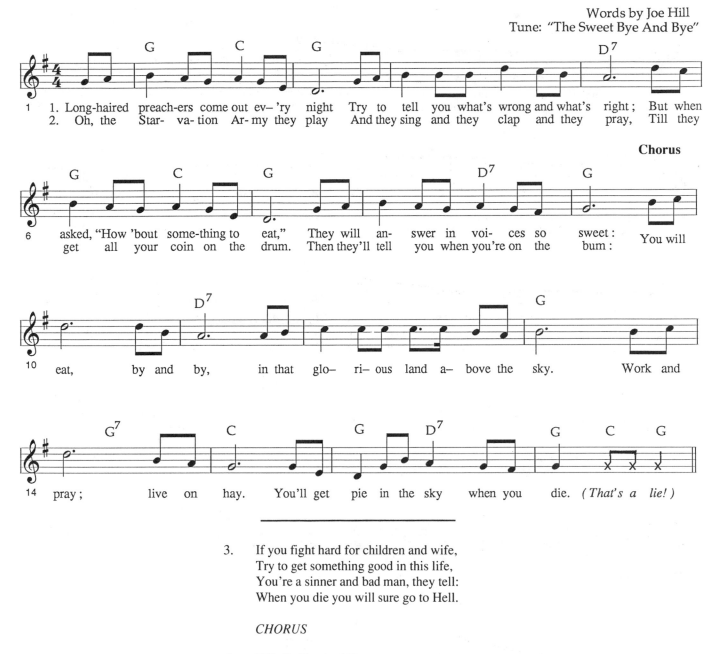

1. Long-haired preach-ers come out ev—'ry night Try to tell you what's wrong and what's right; But when
2. Oh, the Star- va- tion Ar- my they play And they sing and they clap and they pray, Till they

**Chorus**

asked, "How 'bout some-thing to eat," They will an— swer in voi— ces so sweet : You will
get all your coin on the drum. Then they'll tell you when you're on the bum : You will

eat, by and by, in that glo— ri— ous land a— bove the sky. Work and

pray ; live on hay. You'll get pie in the sky when you die. *(That's a lie!)*

3. If you fight hard for children and wife,
   Try to get something good in this life,
   You're a sinner and bad man, they tell:
   When you die you will sure go to Hell.

   *CHORUS*

4. Holy Rollers and Jumpers come out
   And they holler, they jump, and they shout.
   "Give your money to Jesus," they say;
   "He will cure all diseases today."

   *CHORUS*

5. Workingmen of all countries, unite.
   Side by side we for freedom will fight.
   When the world and its wealth we have gained,
   To the grafter we will sing this refrain:

   *CHORUS*

Public domain

21

# Solidarity Forever

Words by Ralph Chaplin
Tune : "John Brown's Body"

1. When the un- ion's in- spi- ra- tion through the work- ers' blood shall run, There can
2. They have ta- ken un- told mill- ions that they ne- ver toiled to earn, But with—

be no pow- er great- er an- y— where be- neath the sun, Yet what
out our brain and mus- cle not a sin- gle wheel could turn. We can

force on earth is weak- er than the fee- ble strength of one? But the
break their haugh- ty pow- er, gain our free- dom when we learn That the

un- ion makes us strong.
un- ion makes us strong.

**Chorus**

Sol- i- dar- i— ty for- ev- er ! Sol- i- dar- i- ty for- ev- er !

Sol- i- dar- i- ty for- ev- er, For the un- ion makes us strong !

3. In our hands is placed a power greater than their
      hoarded gold,
   Greater than the might of armies magnified a
      thousandfold.
   We can bring to birth a new world from the ashes
      of the old,
   For the union makes us strong.

*CHORUS*

Public domain

22

# The Sentry

Words and music by
Jim Smith

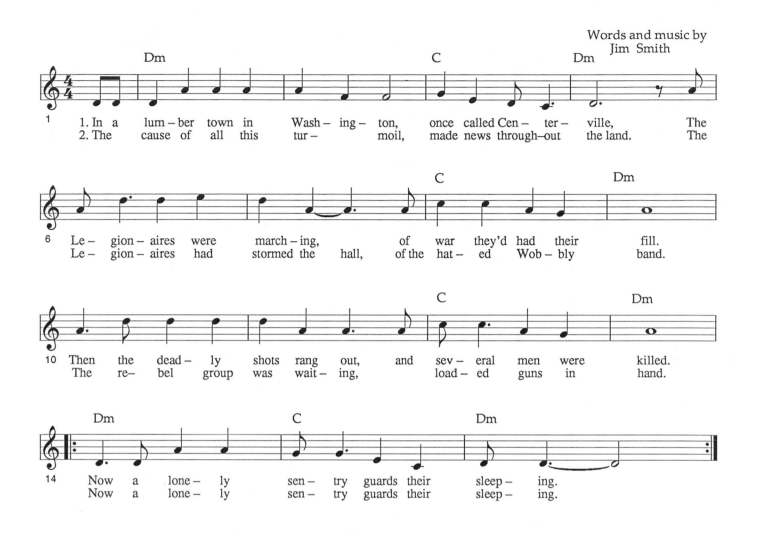

1. In a lum – ber town in Wash – ing – ton, once called Cen – ter – ville, The
2. The cause of all this tur – moil, made news through–out the land. The

Le – gion – aires were march – ing, of war they'd had their fill.
Le – gion – aires had stormed the hall, of the hat – ed Wob – bly band.

Then the dead – ly shots rang out, and sev – eral men were killed.
The re – bel group was wait – ing, load – ed guns in hand.

Now a lone – ly sen – try guards their sleep – ing.
Now a lone – ly sen – try guards their sleep – ing.

2. Angry local citizens soon ran the Wobblies down.
Their leader Wesley Everest was lynched and then cut down.
His bullet riddled body 'neath Hangman's Bridge was found.
Now a lonely sentry guards their sleeping.
Now a lonely sentry guards their sleeping.

3. The rebel group was put on trial and swiftly put away.
Twenty-five to forty years in prison they would pay.
While those who lynched Wes Everest would never serve a day.
Now a lonely sentry guards their sleeping.
Now a lonely sentry guards their sleeping.

4. Some folks say the Wobblies got justice for their crime.
Others say that they were merely victims of the times.
Opposing local businessmen had put them out of line.
Now a lonely sentry guards their sleeping.
Now a lonely sentry guards their sleeping.

5. Today the Centralia Massacre is of the distant past.
The fact that twelve young lives were ruined might be forgot at last.
If not for the sentry who continues at his task.
Silently the sentry guards their sleeping.
Still a lonely sentry guards their sleeping.
Now a lonely sentry guards their sleeping.
Now a lonely sentry guards their sleeping.

23

# Fifty Thousand Lumberjacks

Author : unknown
Tune: "Portland County Jail"

2. Fifty thousand wooden bunks full of things that
crawl;
Fifty thousand restless men have left them once
for all.
One by one they dared not say, "Fat, the hours are
long."
If they did, they'd hike—but now they're fifty
thousand strong.

*CHORUS*

3. Fatty Rich, we know your game, know your pride
is pricked.
Say—but why not be a man, and own when you
are licked?
They've joined the One Big Union—Gee! For
goodness' sake, "Get wise!"
The more you try to buck them now, the more
they organize.

Public domain

*Drawing by Sheryl Stewart.*

*CHORUS*

4. Take a tip and start right in—plan some cozy
     rooms,
   Six or eight spring beds in each, with towels,
     sheets, and brooms;
   Shower baths for men who work keeps them well
     and fit.
   A laundry, too, and drying room, would help a
     little bit.

*CHORUS*

5. Get some dishes, white and clean, good pure food
     to eat.
   See that cook has help enough to keep the table
     neat.
   Tap the bell for eight hours' work; treat the boys
     like men,
   And fifty thousand lumberjacks may come to
     work again.

*CHORUS*

6. Men who work should be well paid. "A man's a
     man for a' that."
   Many a man has a home to keep same as yourself,
     Old Fat.
   Mothers, sisters, sweethearts, wives, children, too,
     galore,
   Stand behind the men to win this bread and butter
     war.

*CHORUS*

# Ballad Of Laura Law

Words and music by
Linda Allen

26

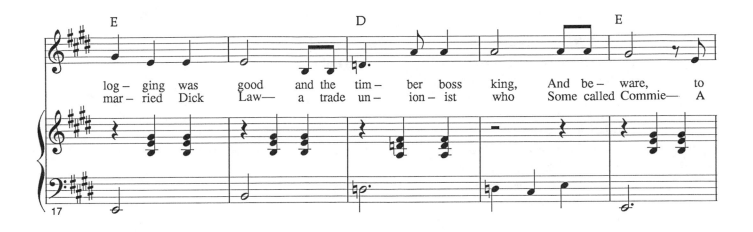

log — ging was good and the tim — ber boss king, And be — ware, to
mar — ried Dick Law — a trade un — ion — ist who Some called Commie— A

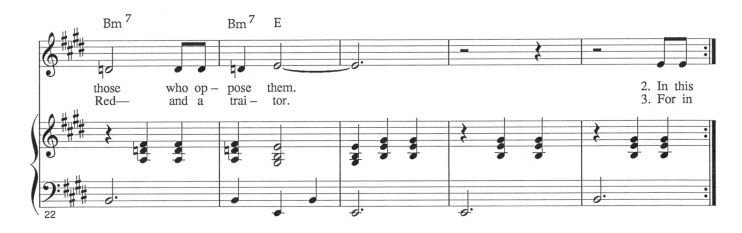

those who op — pose them.
Red— and a trai — tor.

2. In this
3. For in

3. For in Grays Harbor County—a war was declared
Between bosses and labor—and any who dared
Take a stand were called fascists or Commies
and fear
Was the one thing the town held in common.

4. Laura's neighbor recalled the sweet smile in her
voice
As she talked of her son—her three-year-old boy.
How she organized marches of the unemployed
To the steps of the city hall.

5. The reporter then asked, "But was she a Red?"
"She cared little for politics," her neighbor said.
"But she thought folks should have enough bread
No, she wasn't a Red—just a Baptist."

6. In nineteen and forty—a cold winter's night
Laura sat with her needlework next to the light

When a shadow fell over the linen so white
And terror and death filled the room.

7. Her mother found Laura—her screams filled the
air
As she held Laura's body, once gentle and fair
With papers all scattered and blood everywhere.
"Dear God, what has happened here?"

8. Who killed Laura Law? Our ally—our friend?
Some blamed fascists or Reds—no one knew in
the end.
When suspicion and hatred are sown to the wind
The harvest is riot and murder.

9. In Aberdeen town the house still remains
All boarded and still in the cool, cleansing rain
Some walk by and remember the grief and the
shame
And still wonder, who killed Laura Law?

# The Work We Do

*The songs of the working people have always been their sharpest statement, and the one statement that cannot be destroyed. You can burn books, buy newspapers, you can guard against handbills and pamphlets, but you cannot prevent singing. . . . You can learn more about people by listening to their songs than any other way, for into songs go all the hopes and hurts, the angers, fears, the wants and aspirations.*

—John Steinbeck
 *American Folk Songs of Protest*

*I was never in a big stampede because we always caught it in time. . . . The worst time was during thunder. So then we'd whistle and sing to hold them cattle. And long's they could hear you, they wasn't hard to hold. . . . Every cowboy'd have a song of his own like "Hey There, Hi There." Some darned thing. They could see the trouble a-coming and they'd start to singing and whistling.*

—Paul Louden, Okanogan cowman
 *River Pigs and Cayuses*
 *By Ron Strickland*

These are songs about the work we do. The occupations represented reflect Washington's economic base: lumbering, farming, the assembly line, the military. Other songs are about the hard times during the Great Depression when a job couldn't be found.

The apple has been the focus of numerous songs, many celebrating various festivals in the Wenatchee and Yakima areas. **"Apple Picker's Reel,"** inspired by Larry Hanks' two-week stint picking apples in 1966, tells of the beauty of the orchard, along with the discomforts of being an apple picker. It's a great song to keep adding verses to. . . a group of school children added the last verse.

The song **"Down On The Corner (Of Dock and Holly)"** was widely known around Whatcom County during the 1920s. Bellingham streetcars ended their run at the corner of Dock (now Cornwall) and Holly—a location popular with the Salvation Army. The Charley Lind mentioned in the song was a well-known Swedish contractor who lived in a big house in Bellingham's York Addition.

Woody Guthrie arrived at the Bonneville Power Administration's Portland office in the spring of 1941 with his wife, Mary, and his children, looking for a job. He pulled out his guitar, played a few tunes, and was hired as a temporary laborer for one month to write songs promoting the building of the Grand Coulee Dam, for which he'd be paid $266.66. It was the most productive month of Woody Guthrie's life; he wrote twenty-six songs. Guthrie was greatly moved by the migrant workers he met, many of whom were "Okies" who had come from California. The song **"Pastures Of Plenty"** traces the migrant experience through the hard times to the big, green valleys of the Pacific Northwest.

*Promotional brochure courtesy of Special Collections Division, University of Washington Libraries.*

*"Rosies" at the Puget Sound Naval Shipyard, 1919. Courtesy of National Archives.*

The 1973 song **"She'll Never Be Mine"** was written by Bruce "Utah" Phillips. To quote Utah: "It's a boomer's song about silver mining, about farming, about cattle ranching, about the workers creating the wealth and not getting any of it. It's my love song for the country I come from. I've tried to include a lot of the ways I know other people feel about it too."

It is said that during the Depression many penniless men rode for free on the rooftops of trains in order to reach cities or towns where there might be work. A branch of the Kettle Valley Line ran from Spokane into the Kettle Valley in Canada, and the train carried many men who hoped to find work in the valley. **"Kettle Valley Line"** was written around 1952 and is a favorite railroad song among Northwest singers.

During the Second World War many women went to work doing "men's jobs" to help support the war effort. Previously, women had only been employed in "female jobs," working as laundresses or waitresses or perhaps running a boarding house. For the first time women were entering nontraditional jobs. There would be no turning back, even though after the war there was a tremendous propaganda campaign to convince women to go back to their homes. A woman who did a man's job was dubbed "Rosy the riveter." **"Rosy The Riveter—Revisited"** is a tribute to the women of the time, and to many surviving "Rosies."

The military bases of the Northwest have been responsible for the immigration of countless residents to Washington. Many came during or immediately following the Second World War. In many areas the military and related industries remain primary employers. **"Hail, The Navy,"** written by Rosetta Perry Gibbon, was the winner of a "Fleet Week" contest held in 1932 by the Seattle Chamber of Commerce. The song, published in 1933, has been played by U.S. Navy bands around the world as a marching song and has been used as a recruitment song.

Many of Washington's singable folk songs reflect the frustrations of our jobs, as well as the humor and the intense pride we feel. "Working" songs are expressions of our reality as well as of our dreams. Washington workers have much to say about both.

*Asahel Curtis photograph courtesy of Museum of History and Industry.*

*And the day the war ended, every woman in there GOT IT. Leadman came 'round and says, 'Frances, tonight you can hang your torch up, your job's done; the war is over.' And on that day I picked up a piece of scrap iron and lit my torch and wrote my name on it. That was in 1945. This is my proof for my grandchildren and great-grandchildren that I really was a burner in the wartime.*
*—Frances Meskerman*
   *In an interview with Marsha Lash*
   *Washington Women's Heritage*
   *Project*

# Apple Picker's Reel

Words and music by
Larry Hanks

1. Up in the morn–ing be–fore the sun, I don't get home un–til the

**Chorus** Hey, ho, makes you feel so fine, look–ing out a–cross the or–chard in the

day is done, My pick–sack's heavy and my shoul–der's sore, But

bright sun–shine. Hey, ho, makes you feel so free,

I'll be back to–mor–row to pick some more.

stand–ing in the top of an ap–ple tree.

---

*CHORUS*

2.  Start at the bottom and you pick 'em from the
    ground,
    And you pick that tree clean all the way around,
    Then you set up your ladder and you climb up
    high,
    And you're looking through the leaves at the clear
    blue sky.

3.  Three-legged ladder, wobbly as hell,
    Reaching for an apple—whoa! I almost fell,
    Got a 20-pound sack hanging 'round my neck,
    And there's two more apples that I can't quite get.

*FIRST CHORUS*

4.  Well, they come in yellow and green and red,
    And you eat 'em in the mornin' and before you go
    to bed,
    You can play catch if you throw 'em up high,
    Whoops! Squish! Apple pie!

*FINAL CHORUS*

*Hey, ho, you lose your mind,*
*If you sing this song about a hundred times,*
*Hey, ho, you feel so free,*
*Standing in the top of an apple tree.*

# Down On The Corner (Of Dock And Holly)

Author : unknown
Tune : "Reuben, Reuben"

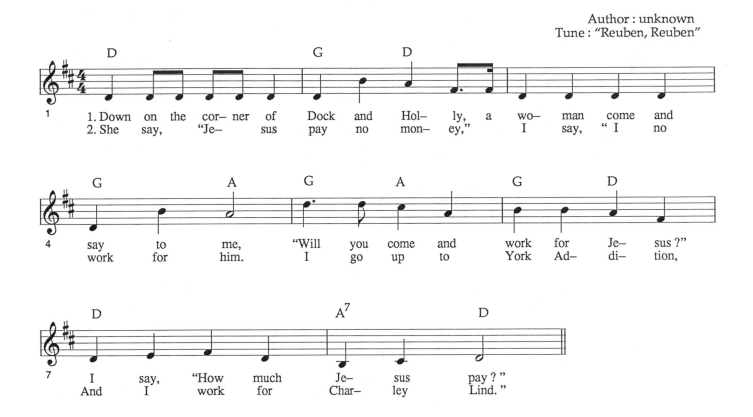

1. Down on the cor— ner of Dock and Hol— ly, a wo— man come and
2. She say, "Je— sus pay no mon— ey," I say, " I no

say to me, "Will you come and work for Je— sus?"
work for him. I go up to York Ad— di— tion,

I say, "How much Je— sus pay ? "
And I work for Char— ley Lind. "

# Pastures Of Plenty

Words and music by
Woody Guthrie

3. California, Arizona, I make all your crops.
Then it's north up to Oregon to gather your hops,
Dig the beets from your ground, cut the grapes
    from your vine
To set on your table your light, sparkling wine.

4. Green pastures of plenty from dry desert ground,
From the Grand Coulee Dam where the waters
    run down,
Every state in the union us migrants has been.
We'll work in this fight, and we'll fight till we
    win.

5. It's always we rambled, that river and I;
All along your green valley I will work till I die.
My land I'll defend with my life if it be,
'Cause my pastures of plenty must always be free.

# She'll Never Be Mine

Words and music by
Bruce Phillips

**CHORUS**

3. My love is Montana and the high Douglas fir,
Many long summers I've labored for her.
My love is the windrows of dry autumn corn
That grew on the land where my children were
born.

4. My love is the life that a boomer will lead,
You have bought her with lies and chained her
with greed.

My love is a dreamer, I follow the dream;
You say she's a beggar, I say she's a queen.

**FINAL CHORUS**

*Someday she'll be mine,*
*Someday she'll be mine,*
*I've won all her treasures so simple and fine,*
*I know someday she'll be mine.*

33

# Kettle Valley Line

Words and music by
Ean Hays

1. I always ride up— on the roof, on the Ket— tle Val— ley
2. I buy a sand— wich from the cook, on the Ket— tle Val— ley

line. I always ride up— on the roof, I could
line. I buy a sand— wich from the cook, he

pay the fare but what's the use? I always ride up—
pock— ets the mon—ey, the dir— ty crook. Oh, I buy a sand— wich

on the roof, on the Ket— tle Val— ley line.
from the cook, on the Ket— tle Val— ley line.

---

3. I order my meals through the ventilator, on the
Kettle Valley line.
I order my meals through the ventilator, on the
Kettle Valley line.
I order my meals through the ventilator, they taste
no worse and saves tippin' the waiter.
Oh, I order my meals through the ventilator, on
the Kettle Valley line.

4. The railway bulls are gentlemen, on the Kettle
Valley line.
The railway bulls are gentlemen, on the Kettle
Valley line.

The railway bulls are gentlemen, we'll never see
their likes again.
Oh, the railway bulls are gentlemen, on the Kettle
Valley line.

5. They tip their hats and call you sir, on the Kettle
Valley line.
They tip their hats and call you sir, on the Kettle
Valley line.
They tip their hats and call you sir, then toss you
in the local stir.
Oh, they tip their hats and call you sir, on the
Kettle Valley line.

# Rosy The Riveter — Revisited

Words and music by
Linda Allen

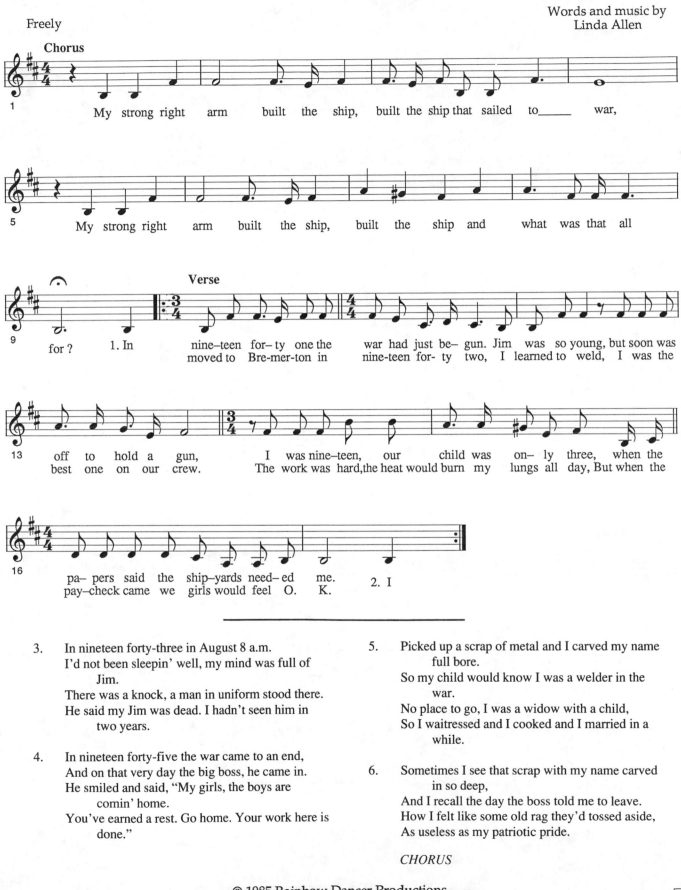

Freely

**Chorus**

1. My strong right arm built the ship, built the ship that sailed to____ war,

5. My strong right arm built the ship, built the ship and what was that all

9. for ?

**Verse**

1. In nine–teen for–ty one the war had just be–gun. Jim was so young, but soon was
moved to Bre–mer–ton in nine-teen for–ty two, I learned to weld, I was the

13. off to hold a gun, I was nine–teen, our child was on–ly three, when the
best one on our crew. The work was hard, the heat would burn my lungs all day, But when the

16. pa– pers said the ship–yards need–ed me.   2. I
pay–check came we girls would feel O. K.

3. In nineteen forty-three in August 8 a.m.
   I'd not been sleepin' well, my mind was full of
      Jim.
   There was a knock, a man in uniform stood there.
   He said my Jim was dead. I hadn't seen him in
      two years.

4. In nineteen forty-five the war came to an end,
   And on that very day the big boss, he came in.
   He smiled and said, "My girls, the boys are
      comin' home.
   You've earned a rest. Go home. Your work here is
      done."

5. Picked up a scrap of metal and I carved my name
      full bore.
   So my child would know I was a welder in the
      war.
   No place to go, I was a widow with a child,
   So I waitressed and I cooked and I married in a
      while.

6. Sometimes I see that scrap with my name carved
      in so deep,
   And I recall the day the boss told me to leave.
   How I felt like some old rag they'd tossed aside,
   As useless as my patriotic pride.

*CHORUS*

# Hail, The Navy

Words and music by
Rosetta Perry Gibbon

On the blue At— lan—tic and the Pa— cif— ic, _____

Ships and subs and car—ri— ers so ter— rif— ic, Are keep—ing us se— cure, of

Our Red White and Blue. _____ HO, THE NA— VY!
We put out to sea. _____ HO, THE NA— VY!

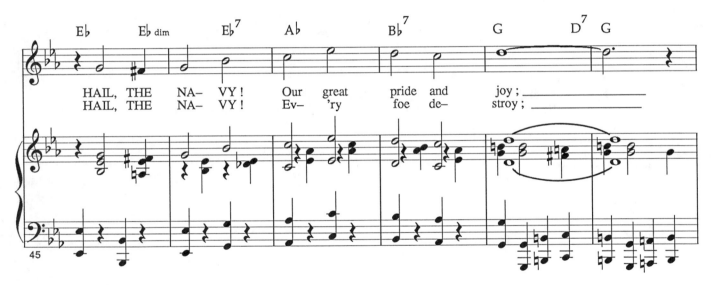

HAIL, THE NA— VY! Our great pride and joy; _____
HAIL, THE NA— VY! Ev— 'ry foe de— stroy; _____

Ne— ver lose her One plane or cruis— er; Na— vy ship a—
Not a sail— or Will ev— er fail her; Na— vy ship a—

# The Frozen Logger

The songs, poems, and stories of the Northwest loggers are part of a tradition that goes back to the beginnings of logging in the state. Loggers often sang songs and recited poetry to relieve the boredom and tension that filled their everyday lives, and this remained a regular form of entertainment well into the 1950s. The songs of the logger deal with the dangers of the profession, the laughable ignorance of the greenhorn, the reputation for toughness that loggers have earned, or the meddlesome intransigence of bureaucracy.

Many times, stories were set to music in the logging camps. James Stevens, the author of *Paul Bunyan,* worked in Washington lumber camps as a young man and listened to the loggers spin their yarns. He wrote **"The Frozen Logger"** based on his experiences.

Helen Davis is best known as the composer of "Washington, My Home." What is not so well known is that she has also composed numerous songs based on Washington legends and stories. **"Wet Me Down In Washington"** is taken from the official Territorial Centennial play for the state of Washington, "Eliza and the Lumberjack." The musical, which includes sixteen songs written by Davis, was produced at St. Martin's College in Olympia in 1953 and performed twenty-three times around the state.

Buzz Martin, the "Singing Logger," was the acknowledged grand master of logger songs. According to his daughter, Judy Janes, he not only "worked every job in the woods, from whistle punk to hooktender, he also put down in song the customs, joys, and woes of a logger life style . . . he could work a hard day in the woods getting wet and muddy with the best of them, then step on stage and capture an audience's heart and create smiles with his dynamic style and true to life songs" (*Loggers World,* April 1986). Buzz was an Oregonian, but he also lived and worked in the northeastern Cascades and on the Olympic Peninsula. **"Fire Danger"** is a song Buzz wrote about the frustrations of the logger who is shut down due to "fire danger"—a theme often repeated in other logger poems and songs.

Logger poetry, like logger music, has been around almost as long as logging itself. Old-time loggers whose school days were filled with recitations would repeat the works they'd learned in school as a way to entertain themselves at night. Over the years, the loggers began reciting original works. "Until mass media came along, it was common for working people and men with a capital M to write poems. (Today) poetry has come to be seen as something that's effeminate, so the idea of rough, tough guys writing and reading poetry is rejected by some people. People absolutely refuse to believe it," says Jens Lund, Washington State Folklorist. The poem "Jim Oatfield" by Woodrow "Woody" Gifford, considered to be the dean of Northwest logger poets, is about a real-life Washington logger who achieved legendary status.

*Stevens County logging train. Courtesy of Eastern Washington State Historical Society.*

# Jim Oatfield

The Great Northwest, where the Firs grow
    tall,
There's a logger there who can high lead
    them all—
Bunyan, the Blue Ox, McFilkin and Shield
Were cord wood choppers 'longside Jim
    Oatfield.

Jim is a man with a mighty will,
Who is always in a hurry and never sits
    still
There's no mud hole too oozey or hill too
    steep
To stop Jim Oatfield's pickup or jeep.

In the gray hours of dawn, when the day is
    new,
There's a hum, then a roar as Jim passes
    through—
The Speed Boys patrol from ten to ten;
When they get where they are, that's
    where Jim has been.

From high on top of the K.M. Crest,
Jim's log trucks thunder down four abreast;
They twist and wind 'round the Klint
    Creek Trail
And stand in line at the log dump scale.

The Dumper had his troubles too;
He cursed and swore, and his tin hat
    threw—
Then he yarded it back with a long arm
    sweep
And turned to Jim in his blue green jeep.

"Hell, man, we're plugged from shore to
    shore;
This cussed river won't hold any more—
I've wired the Union for an extra crew,
So shut her down till the bus gets through."

Jim's face lit up and his smile was wide;
"Why, man, we're only runnin' one side—
At midnight we're startin' two sides more
And I'm due in Salt Lake at a quarter to
    four—
So don't stand here, my boy, and cry;
If you can't raft 'em wet, why raft 'em
    dry."
The Northwest Woods have known the
    steel
Of many a cork booted nonpareil;
But 'twould take a logger with a lot of
    know
To pack Jim's Lunchbox on a Hemlock
    Show.

*Log drive in Stevens County.*
*Courtesy of Eastern*
*Washington State Historical*
*Society.*

# The Frozen Logger

Words and music by
James Stevens

1. As I set down one eve— ning in a tim— ber town ca— fe,
For a six foot se— ven wait— ress, to me these words did say.

2. "I see you are a log— ger, and not a com— mon bum,
For no one but a log— ger, stirs his cof— fee with his thumb.

3. "My lover was a logger—there's none like him today—
   If you'd sprinkle whiskey on it, he'd eat a bale of hay.

4. "He never shaved the whiskers from off his horny hide,
   But he'd pound 'em in with a hammer, then bite 'em off inside.

5. "My lover came to see me one freezing winter day,
   He held me in a fond embrace that broke three vertebrae.

6. "He kissed me when we parted so hard he broke my jaw,
   And I could not speak to tell him he'd forgot his mackinaw.

7. "I watched my logger lover going through the snow,
   A-sauntering gaily homeward at forty-eight below.

8. "The weather tried to freeze him, it tried its level best—
   At one hundred degrees below zero he buttoned up his vest.

9. "It froze clean down to China, it froze to the stars above.
   At one thousand degrees below zero, it froze my logger love.

10. "They tried in vain to thaw him, and if you'll believe me, sir,
    They made him into ax blades, to chop the Douglas fir.

11. "That's how I lost my lover, and to this cafe I come,
    And here I wait till someone stirs his coffee with his thumb.

12. "And then I tell my story, of my love they could not thaw,
    Who kissed me when we parted, so hard he broke my jaw."

# Wet Me Down In Washington

Words and music by Helen Davis
From the musical "Eliza and the Lumberjack"

43

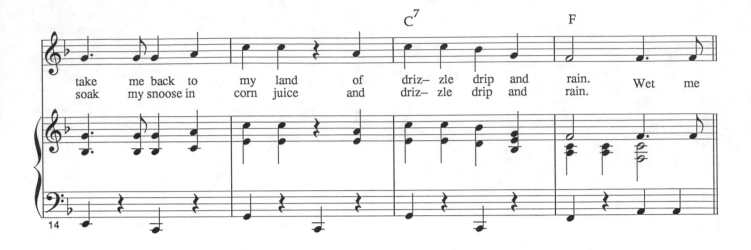

take me back to my land of driz—zle drip and rain. Wet me
soak my snoose in corn juice and driz—zle drip and rain.

**Chorus**

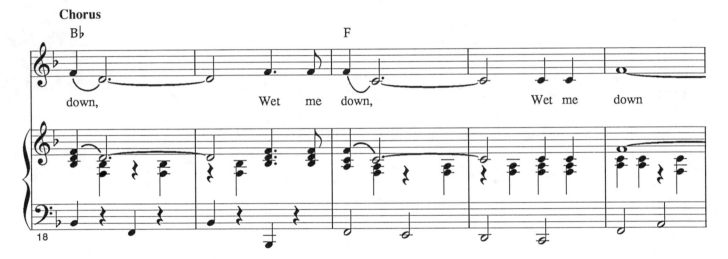

down, Wet me down, Wet me down

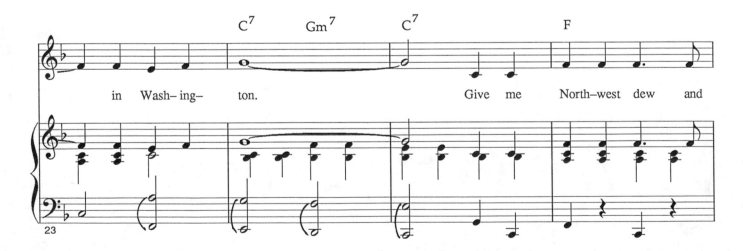

in Wash—ing—ton. Give me North—west dew and

driz– zle, fog so thick you need a chi– sel, Wet me down,

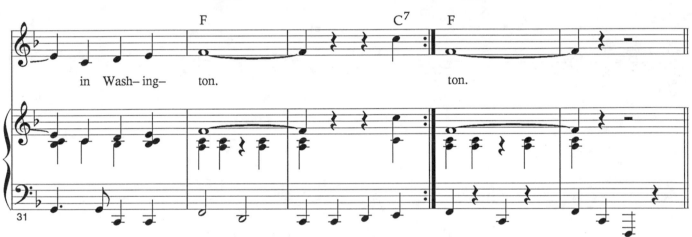

in Wash–ing– ton. ton.

*CHORUS*

3. I'd limb your widow-maker—I'd kick off every
    knot.
I'll do it with my two bare feet from butt end to
    the top,
Won't cuss the old boss logger for all this sweat
    and pain,
Just sprinkle me with whiskey, my drizzle drip
    and rain.

*CHORUS*

4. I'll shoulder up my peavey, I'll pull that log alone,
I'll send her down the old skid road, just leave the
    bulls at home.
I'll roll her in the river, no tug, no grunt, no strain.
So kindly pass the bottle, our drizzle drip and rain.

*CHORUS*

# Fire Danger

Words and music by
Buzz Martin

1. I'm just a poor old gyp–po log–ger, Try–in' to make ends meet, Got e–quip–ment I got–ta pay for And a fa-mi-ly that's got–ta eat, But these guys from the For– est Ser– vice, Ev– 'ry time they come a– round, All they do is look for some–thing wrong, So they can close you down.

*Other verses*

2. These pink cheeked boys from the mid–dle east, It's the first time they've seen a tree, Yet they know more a–bout log–ging Than an old tim–ber beast like me, They've

3. Some–how I made it thru the win–ter months, fight–in' mud and sleet and snow, Now good wea– ther's fi–nal–ly here and I ought ta make some dough, But the

46

**28** gone to col— lege and they've learned how To tie rib— bons all a— round, And

**32** look up in their rule book, For a way to close you down.

**Chorus**

**36** We got— ta close you down, Fire dan— ger all a— round,

**40** Right here, you see on page twen— ty three, We got— ta close you down.

**44** Right here, you see on page twen— ty three, we got— ta close you down.

3.  Somehow I made it through the winter months,
    Fightin' mud and sleet and snow,
    Now good weather's finally here,
    And I oughta make some dough.
    But the Forest Service is checkin' now,
    And you oughta see 'em frown,
    I bet they've already found a dozen ways
    They can close me down.

4.  When them boys live their life spans out,
    And they meet their judgment day,
    If they make it on up to heaven, well,
    I guess they'll be OK.
    But if they go the other direction,
    They'll take one look around,
    And say, "Satan, look at the Fire Danger,
    We gotta close you down."

*CHORUS*

47

# From the Mountains to the Sea

Many of Washington's songs are inspired by the outstanding physical features of the state's landscape. This is the palette upon which we do our best work. For many of our people, the mountains and the sea stir the imagination and bring forth strong artistic expressions.

Harold Weeks, who along with Oliver Wallace wrote "Hindustan," featured in chapter eight, was one of Seattle's first and most famous composers of national hits. The last song Weeks wrote was **"Little Cabin In The Cascade Mountains,"** which was recorded in 1930 by country singers Carson Robison and Bud Billings.

Michael Tomlinson's **"The Climb"** was the most requested song on Seattle's radio station KEZX in 1982. The song sold thousands of copies, with proceeds going to the Northwest Handicapped Supports and Recreation Association. The song is about amputee Don Bennett, who on July 15, 1982, reached the summit of 14,410-foot high Mount Rainier, becoming the first amputee in the world to do so. Don was picked as one of the "Sports Stars of the Year" by the *Seattle Post-Intelligencer* in 1982.

The eruption of Mount Saint Helens in 1980 brought forth more songs than any single event in Washington's recent history . . . songs that captured the mystery, the tragedy, and sometimes even the humor of the cataclysmic event.

Tom Shindler, a geology student and lover of mountains, was involved in search and rescue efforts following the May 18, 1980, eruption. When the second explosion occurred on May 25, Tom described it as "the darkest morning I'd ever seen, and one of the weirdest thunderstorms occurred that night. An army officer reported that his helicopters were grounded, and 'it's raining mud.' " Tom wrote **"The Giants Are Only Asleep"** as a reminder that people can never be too sure about what lies under all that snow.

A number of songs written about the eruption focused on the legendary man of the mountain, Harry Truman, who refused to leave his home. Harry told a *Portland Oregonian* reporter that "if the mountain goes then I'll go with it." Bellingham songwriter Tom Hunter was inspired by the article to write **"Harry Truman"** as a tribute to the old man who

*The former beauty of Mount Saint Helens, captured by Asahel Curtis. Courtesy of Special Collections Division, University of Washington Libraries.*

*This 1913 photo shows workers unloading their catch from a fish trap, a mode of harvesting salmon later made illegal. Courtesy of Library of Congress.*

wouldn't come down off the mountain.

**"I Like Humpback Salmon,"** sung to the tune of "I Like Mountain Music," is a favorite of Northwest fishermen. It seems to have gained the status of a true folk song—it grew out of the fishing community and has "spawned" many local variations. A variation heard by Jens Lund was sung by Charlie Nelson, a Haida fisherman from Alaska. Rather than singing "good Swede fishermen" Nelson sang "caught by the crew of the *Cheryl Ann*."

> I like humpback salmon
> Good old humpback salmon
> Caught by the good Swede fishermen
> I like crabs and shellfish
> Good old crabs and shellfish
> Caught by the good Swede fishermen
> I like T-bone steak
> From the state of Texas
> But give me fish
> And I don't care if I do pay taxes
> I like humpback salmon
> Good old humpback salmon
> Caught by the good Swede fishermen
> —To the tune of "I Like Mountain
> Music"

Shipwrecks have stirred songwriters in Washington from earliest times, and contemporary fishermen have the same dread of shipwrecks that their forebears did. During the summer of 1969 Robert Rohde survived the sinking of the boat he was crewing on, and he wrote the song **"Silver Tip"** about his experience.

Ferries provide a popular theme for Northwest songwriters. Everett songwriter John Dwyer wrote "Notice To Mariners," which concerns a historical event based on the fact that early navigation was dependent upon the use of echoes. Some rocks and points of land had echoboards to reflect the sound of boat whistles.

*If a whistle sound hit a solid wall, the echo would bounce back sharply. If it hit a ragged hillside, the echo was apt to sound just as ragged.*

*Even though captains revere the old steam whistle, they admit that a well designed airhorn gives a sharper echo. Now, with the use of radar, there is less need for echo navigation, but many captains still use echoes from their whistles (airhorn or steam) for dead reckoning.*

*—Morris H. Pixley*
*Ferry Tales From Puget Sound*
*By Joyce Delbridge*

The beauty, power, and romance of Washington's natural environment are sources of inspiration for songwriters. So let the music carry you—from the mountains to the sea.

# Little Cabin In The Cascade Mountains

Words and music by
Harold Weeks

50

51

where I long to be   Where the tall   trees frown,   and the  streams come tumb-ling down   and the

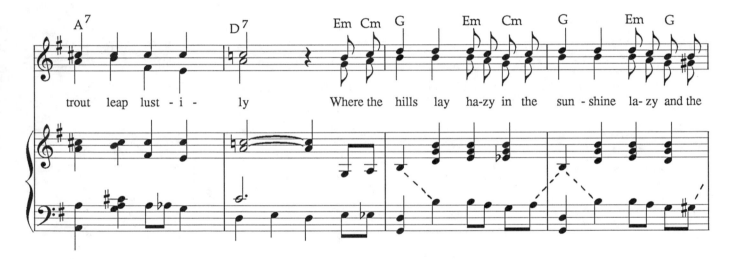

trout leap lust - i -   ly      Where the  hills  lay  ha-zy in the   sun - shine  la- zy and the

day  ends peace-ful - ly      Oh that lit - tle  cab- in in the    Cas- cade Moun-tains, it's a

par - a - dise to me. There's a me. ____

# The Climb

Verses 1 & 2

Words and music by
Michael Tomlinson

1. Up ev'ry morn-ing the break of day his face was wrink-led and his hair was gray,
2. Four long miles and more to go he knew he could make it if he just went slow

You ne-ver know how long a man is stay-ing _____
Some times it's hard to keep be– liev–in'. _____

Don-ald made his
But this time he was

dai- ly rounds thru' the mea-dow and o-ver in- to high- er ground past where the
bound to fly and he prac– ticed hard as the days went by you could hear his

neigh-bor- hood kids were play– ing _____
strong and stead– y breath– in' _____

And the words I know he said
(2x) As he turned to his friends

**Chorus**

I will climb that ho-ly mount– ain ____ in the hours of the day Let it

drain my stur– dy bo– dy as it may, ____ I have worked long and

54

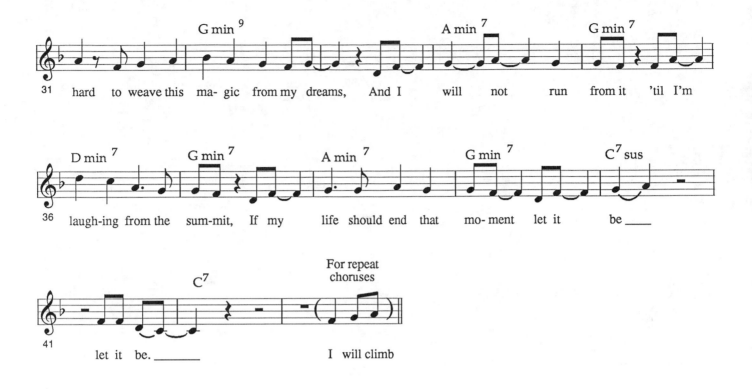

G min 9      A min 7      G min 7

31   hard   to weave this ma- gic from my dreams,   And I   will   not   run   from it   'til I'm

D min 7      G min 7      A min 7      G min 7      C7 sus

36   laugh-ing from the   sum-mit,   If my   life should end that   mo- ment let it   be ____

For repeat choruses

C7

41   let it   be. _____      I will climb

_____

3.   Seven kids, a faithful wife
   They loved their daddy, and they all knew why
   He had to try to climb that field again
   The northern face of Mount Rainier
   He had to make it 'cause he failed last year
   Up where the weather stills all seasons.

   Now most of us will never know
   The sound of a mountain in the freezing cold
   And how hard it is to keep on climbin'
   He just had to listen from the mountain top
   Tho' his leg was missing, well, he still moved up
   And everybody knew the man could make it
   As he turned to his friends
   And the words, I know he said,

   *REPEAT CHORUS THREE TIMES*

# The Giants Are Only Asleep

Words and music by
Tom Shindler

56

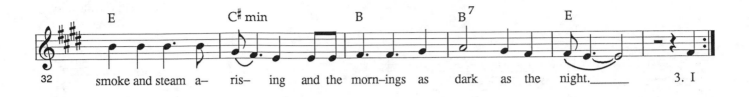

32     smoke and steam a— ris— ing and the morn–ings as dark as the night._____     3. I

3.    I woke to explosions and rattling windows
One morning, the eighteenth of May.
It was hard to believe when they said she had
       blown,
I could hear it from so far away.

4.    But the radio told us it all was for real,
That the Mountain had met with her fate,
And the ash cloud was spreading to blot out the
       sun
And bury one half of the state.

*CHORUS*

5.    INSTRUMENTAL VERSE

6.    The mud flowed down the Toutle, the Cowlitz and
       Columbia
Washing out the bridges on its way.
Closing roads and cities and scaring politicians,
The mountain filled the headlines every day.

*CHORUS*

7.    Is it really any wonder when you hear the
       mountains thunder
Just like they've done so many times before?
Funny, how so many folks were taken by surprise,
Like volcanoes never happen anymore.

8.    Those lovely white snow peaks, those rulers of
       mountains,
Who knows what secrets they keep?
But when they look like forever, just stop and
       remember
The Giants are only asleep.

# Harry Truman
## (Of Mount Saint Helens)

Words and music by
Tom Hunter

**Verse**

1. He had lived up there since 'twen-ty-nine, Run a lodge and
2. He said "The earth-quake scared me bad up here, But I've walked this moun-tain for

filled his time drink-in' whis-ky rais-in' cats and tell-ing big tall tales.
fif-ty years and it ain't gon-na get me if the damn thing ev-er blows.

And now the moun-tain home he had, Was shak-ing like the
Be-sides I've got food, four weeks sup-ply, And whis-key, no, I'll

earth gone mad, When they warned him, he said "No, I think I'll stay."
ne-ver run dry. I am this moun-tain, you can ask her, she knows."

**Chorus**

If the moun-tain goes Then I'll go with it.

If the moun-tain goes I'll go a-long. If the moun-tain goes

58

26 Then I'll go with it. I'm gon— na

30 stay right here 'cause here's where I be— long.

---

*CHORUS*

3.   Then on May eighteenth, Saint Helens blew
     It tore the mountain right in two,
     With trees ripped up, clouds of ash, the earth was
              glowing red.
     As for Harry, no one knows,
     He's up there still so the legend goes,
     While the newspapers list him missing, presumed
              dead.

4.   Now some say death's like going home
     How the worst fate is to die alone,
     Far from the people and the places you have
              known.
     Maybe that's why Harry wouldn't leave,
     It doesn't really matter what we believe,
     Whether dead or alive old Harry's still at home.

# Silver Tip

Words and music by
Robert Rohde

20 know that now for sure. There were a mil— lion ships that made that trip,

24 Why'd I have to get a— board her? Why'd I have to get a— board her?

---

*CHORUS*

3. Ray kept us busy those first few days, tho' there
    was no work to be done;
He just took it on himself to see we didn't have no
    fun.
And Bob and I worked in the rain, and did we
    moan and cuss;
And we nicknamed Ray by the second day as Ray
    the Superfluous.

*CHORUS*

4. Then on the second night as I did lie in the
    fo'c'sle fast asleep,
The skipper came and called my name and yanked
    me to my feet.
Then he shook me up, and called me a pup, and a
    worthless lackin' lump.
Then he told me to get my butt upstairs and man
    that ship's bilge pump.

*SECOND CHORUS*

*Oh that Silver Tip, she was a sinking ship, I know
    that now for sure.
There were a million ships that made that trip,
Why'd I have to get aboard her?
Why'd I have to get aboard her?*

5. So I was outside pumpin' with all my strength,
    tryin' to keep that boat afloat,
When my sidekick Bob, with an awful sob, just
    fell clean off that boat.
And I watched him as he went down once, and I
    watched him go down again,
Then I recalled three times is all they allow to
    drownin' men.

*CHORUS*

6. So I reached out and I grabbed Bob's hand, and I
    pulled him back on board,
Do you think he said thanks to me, no he just
    thanked the Lord.
But I didn't have time right then to mention
    impropriety,
Because the Silver Tip she was a-sinkin' low,
    bein' covered by the sea.

*CHORUS*

7. So I went back to pump some more, tho' I saw
    that it was no use,
Then the skipper yelled for me to go and get that
    seine skiff loose.
So I was back there standin' on the stern, tryin to
    get those chains undone,
And we just sank into the sea just like the settin'
    sun.

*CHORUS*

8. So I took off a'swimmin' for the cabin roof, seine
    net floatin' all around,
With all the clothes that I had on, it was a a
    wonder that I didn't drown.
But just when I thought that I would drown,
    someone pulled me from the sea,
And I knew it was true, if I hadn't saved Bob, he
    wouldn't be there now savin' me.

*CHORUS*

*REPEAT FIRST VERSE*

# Notice To Mariners

Words and music by
John Dwyer

1. Come all you North—west sail—ors, who____ cruise on Pu—get Sound, And
2. The fer—ry left Se—at—tle, 'twas____ on a fog—gy day, The

list—en to my sto—ry, for well it will a—stound; 'Tis
cap—tain had no wor—ries, for well he knew the way; He

of a fer—ry cap—tain, who ven—tured forth one day, And
head—ed 'cross the wa—ter, where fin—ny things a—bound, And

of the fate be—fell him, as he sailed on the bay.
set his course for Bre—mer—ton, a—cross famed Pu—get Sound.

3. He left Seattle Harbor, and passed Duwamish
     Head,
   Past Alki on the port side, he westerly did head;
   And now 'twas open water, across to Orchard
     Point,
   Through fog as thick as chowder, the ferry's bow
     did point.

4. Now all good skippers have a trick, who sail these
     waters 'round,
   And when the fog is thickest, 'tis then they steer
     by sound;
   Full several times a minute, their whistle loud
     they blow,
   And by the echo bouncing, when land is close
     they know.

5. The ferry neared Rich Passage, a place of rocks
     and shoals,
   And narrow as an hourglass, as past Point White
     she goes;
   The captain slowed the ferry, and not to run
     aground,
   He blew upon his whistle, and listened for the
     sound.

6. Now, a farmer on Point Glover, across the neck
     from White,
   Had tied his cow that foggy morn, upon lush grass
     to bite;
   So several times a minute, the ferry's whistle blew,
   And as the captain listened, the echo came back
     "Moo!"

7. The captain turned the vessel, still steering by the
     sound,
   And guided by that silly cow, the ferry ran
     aground;
   So all you Northwest sailors, give listen to me
     now,
   And when you cruise on Puget Sound, don't
     navigate by cow!

# Ya Do the Hokey-Pokey

Washington songwriters have been responsible for some of the best-loved children's songs in America. But this chapter is not just for children—everyone will find a favorite here.

Perhaps the best-known children's song is **"The Hokey-Pokey."** The music was written in 1947 by the Sun Valley Trio—Tafft Baker, Larry LaPrise, and Charles Macak. The words were written by Tafft Baker, who tried the song out on his girlfriend, Jean. A year later they married, the song was recorded, and the two of them traveled around the country promoting the song. "The Hokey-Pokey" is so well-known that it is often considered "traditional" and has been a favorite of children for generations.

**"The Gooey Duck Song"** has become a Northwest favorite with adults and children

*The Evergreen State College mascot. Drawing by Sheryl Stewart.*

alike. The geoduck (pronounced gooey-duck), a giant clam with a long "neck," is highly prized by Northwest clam diggers. A Japanese version of "The Gooey Duck Song" sold thousands of records in that country and the song was also a big hit in Australia. The popularity of "The Gooey Duck Song" has inspired gooey duck dolls, coloring books, and T-shirts. The elusive creature is also the mascot of The Evergreen State College in Olympia.

From 1955 until 1967 Stan Boreson hosted KING-TV's "Klubhouse Show," an afternoon children's program with the lazy Basset hound, No Motion, and Stan's alter egos: Uncle Torval, Aunt Torval, and the Japanese chef, Sam Samoto. The theme song for the show, **"Zero Dacus,"** became as familiar to Northwest children and their parents as "It's Howdy Doody Time!" and Ovaltine.

*Stan Boreson, host of KING-TV's "Klubhouse Show." Courtesy of Stan Boreson.*

Around 1980 the apple maggot arrived in Washington, posing a serious economic threat to fruit growers around the state. In 1985 regulations aimed at preventing the spread of the apple maggot by artificial means were adopted, and signs were posted around the state by the Department of Agriculture and the Department of Transportation. Seattle songwriter Mark Cohen made the words from the sign into a round, the **"Apple Maggot Quarantine Round,"** which is, fortunately, spreading more rapidly than the maggot.

Music by Mark Cohen

Ap– ple mag– got qua–ran–tine a– re– a Do not trans– port home– grown fruit.

© 1986 Mark Cohen.

One of the best-known Jewish children's songs in North America was co-written by Samuel Goldfarb and his brother, Israel. Samuel grew up on the sidewalks of New York's East Side—a contemporary of George Gershwin and Irving Berlin, both of whom he knew. He earned his college tuition playing the piano and organ in silent film houses in Tin Pan Alley. He moved to Seattle in 1930 and became the musical director of Seattle's Temple DeHirsch. While serving as director he composed hundreds of children's songs, including **"My Dreydl,"** which was adopted by the Seattle Public Schools to be sung during Hanukkah. Another of Goldfarb's songs, "Shalom Aleichem," appears in chapter seven.

The tradition of the dreydl goes back to the period before the first Hanukkah was celebrated over two thousand years ago. During the time when the Jews were dominated by Syria, practicing Judaism and learning to read and write Hebrew were punishable by death. Jewish children devised a method to teach each other how to read right under the noses of the Syrians. They used small clay tops—dreydls—inscribed around the top with the letters of the Hebrew language to teach the "alef bet" (alphabet), thus retaining their sense of cultural identity during a period of oppression. The dreydl has remained an important symbol of freedom among the Jewish people.

Washington songs have for years delighted children around the world and have added greatly to our cultural identity. Now everybody stand up . . . put your hands on your hips . . ."You put your right hand in . . ."

# The Hokey-Pokey

Words and music by
Tafft Baker

1. You put your right hand in, You put your right hand out, You put your right hand in and you shake it all a-bout, you do the ho-key-po-key, and you turn your-self a-round,
(bend elbows, point index fingers up, sway hips)

That's what it's all a-bout!
(clap in rhythm)

# The Gooey Duck Song

By R. Konzak and
J. Elfendahl

1.You can hear the dig-gers say as they're head-ed for the bay, Oh I got-ta dig a duck, got-ta
2.Oh it takes a lot of luck and a cer-tain kind of pluck, Just to dig a-round the muck just to

dig a duck a day, 'cuz I get a buck a duck: If I dig a duck a day so I
get a goo-ey duck, Well he has-n't got a front and he has-n't got a back, he___

got-ta dig a duck got-ta dig a duck a day.
does-n't know Don-ald and he does-n't go___ "Quack".

Dig a duck, dig a duck

dig a goo-ey duck, Dig a duck dig a goo-ey duck, Dig a duck a day.

*A clam this ugly at least deserves a "catchy" song. Courtesy of Special Collections Division, University of Washington Libraries.*

# Zero Dacus

Words by Elliot Brown
Tune : Traditional

Public domain

# My Dreydl

Words by S. S. Grossman
Music by S. E. Goldfarb

1. I have a lit– tle drey– dl, I made it out of clay, And when it's dry and read– y, Then drey– dl I shall play. Oh drey– dl, drey– dl, drey– dl, I made it out of clay; Oh drey– dl, drey– dl, drey– dl, Now read– y I shall play.

**Shǐn** (Sheen) — Put some back.

**Hay** — Take half of the pot.

**Gimmel** — Take all of the pot.

**Nŏŏn** (Nun) — Take nothing.

2. It has a lovely body,
   With leg so short and thin;
   And when it is all tired,
   It drops and then I win.
   Oh dreydl, dreydl, dreydl,
   With leg so short and thin;
   Oh dreydl, dreydl, dreydl,
   It drops and then I win.

3. My dreydl, always playful,
   It loves to dance and spin.
   A happy game of dreydl,
   Come play, now let's begin.
   Oh dreydl, dreydl, dreydl,
   It loves to dance and spin.
   Oh dreydl, dreydl, dreydl,
   Come play, now let's begin.

Public domain

68

# Lovin', Fightin', Drinkin', and Prayin': Songs of Passion

In this chapter are songs representing some of Washington residents' deepest, most heartfelt emotions. These are songs of love, of faith, of loyalty to friends and alma mater.

**"Northwest Gal"** is a salty tribute to the woman of the Pacific Northwest, a woman as strong and independent as any man. Bob Nelson has penned a poem for the male counterpart of the Northwest gal. One verse reads:

What is a Puget Sounder, I'll tell you if I
  can
He's a rugged individual, a special breed
  of man.
He doesn't shave, his clothes are old,
He lives down on the beach,
Where all of God's gifts to man
Are there within his reach.

The Alaska-Yukon-Pacific Exposition, held to commemorate the Yukon gold rush, took place in Seattle in 1909. The Ashford Collection at the University of Washington's Music Library holds numerous songs written for the event. **"I Will See You In Seattle, Celia Mine"** represents many of the ideals so common to the age—boosterism, new opportunity, the idealization of capitalism—in striking contrast to the militant labor songs being written then. But it's primarily a love song, and that story remains universal.

**"The Cougar Fight Song"**—the Washington State University fight song—was written by two members of the class of 1919. Following the First World War (and a 1916 win in the Rose Bowl over Brown University), student leaders and faculty at what was then Washington State College wanted to rebuild student spirit and gain student support for the sports teams. The president of the student body, Ward Rinehart, asked two music majors, Phyllis Sayles and Zella Melcher, to write a fast-paced fight song. The two women did such a good job that the song has remained unchanged for sixty-nine years.

In the fall of 1915 *The University of Washington Daily* printed the following ad: "Twenty Five Dollars for New Washington Song Awaits Successful Student in *Daily* Contest . . . Song and Yells Needed for California Games—Contributions Must Be In By October 22."

A young student of the class of '16 named Lester J. Wilson rose to the challenge, capturing the school's fighting spirit in a marching song that remains a classic. In a 1961 newspaper article Lester remembered the writing of the song:

*When the contest was launched, I found myself sort of stunned in the face of an opportunity I wasn't sure I could measure up to. But ten days later, with gentle but persistent urging on the part of Pauline [his wife], I came up with the chorus, 'Heaven help the foes of Washington.' Next came* **'Bow Down To Washington'** *as my title.*

*At this point, the real trouble started! Many of our friends heard about the competition and came to our apartment to join in the singing of the then fragmentary 'Bow Down.' The singing went on into the wee hours of the morning.*

*The neighbors in and near our apartment became incensed at the nightly repetition. They phoned the manager of our apartment, they phoned us, and finally, two policemen arrived with an official complaint.*

*After the officers learned what was up, they stayed on to help us sing the song.*

For pure passion and fervor, few songs can match those sung by the Women's Christian

*Clandestine beer party, Seattle, 1931. E. H. Curtis photograph courtesy of Rod Slemmons Collection.*

Temperance Union. **"Cold Water,"** collected by Paul Ashford, dates back to the 1870s. It represents the ideals of the Prohibition movement as the women of the WCTU sought to save people from the evils of alcohol. Ashford's mother was an ardent supporter of the WCTU, and he was fascinated by the songs that came out of that movement. To his mother's dismay, he was equally intrigued with classic drinking songs. He put them together in a book of temperance and drinking songs called *High and Dry.* Unfortunately, the book wasn't published before Ashford's death, but he did leave behind the Ashford Collection, a wonderful collection of sheet music at the Music Library of the University of Washington.

Songs of faith constitute a large segment of Washington's musical heritage. After all, religious songs were the only acceptable form of music for many of the settlers who came to Washington Territory in the 1800s. Chapter one contains " Missionary's Farewell," a classic

hymn of its time, and in chapter two there are examples of hymns altered to fit the message of the Wobblies. But as in other categories of Washington music, diversity is the common denominator. **"Shalom Aleichem,"** one of the best-loved songs in Jewish tradition, is known throughout the world. The words were written by Samuel Goldfarb and his brother Israel. Another song written by Samuel Goldfarb, "My Dreydl," appears in chapter six.

From Prohibition to true love, from school spirit to religious fervor— Washingtonians express themselves easily in song. Love songs capture some of the special qualities that make the Northwest man or woman unique. Washington songs of faith reflect the broad diversity that is so characteristic of the state. And many a fan has ardently rooted for the home team. The songs in this chapter, like so many others, reveal the depth of feelings that flow in the hearts of Washington residents. They are songs to be sung with passion.

# Northwest Gal

Words and music by
Susy McAleer

1. Don't you mar-ry a South-ern girl, mag-no-lias in her hair_____. Who
2. Don't you mar-ry a col-lege girl, with ed-u-ca-tion fine_____. For
3. Don't you mar-ry an Eas-tern girl, with skin of peaches and cream _____. For the

does-n't know a sockeye from a big-mouth bass, and does-n't e-ven care, But
e-very____ time__ you__ catch a fish, she'll moan and start to cryin'. But
o-cean __ wind__ will__ bleach it white and the mold will turn it green. But

mar-ry a gal who can bait a hook and knows just how to swear_____, Who'll
mar-ry a gal with a strong right arm who can wield a club of pine_____, And
mar-ry a lass with__ sea-weed hair, who's mu-scled, long and lean _____, With a

stand straight up on her two webbed feet, and treat you fair and square !
smash that fish right be-tween his eyes____, each and ever-y time !
skin like fine old ____ lea-ther, tanned, and a gaze so straight and keen !

**Chorus**

A North-west gal can swat a flea, or shoot a bear, Or chop a tree. She's

got webbed feet like you and me ; She's the mate for you, my son !

71

# I Will See You In Seattle, Celia Mine

Words and music by
Robert Elwell

1. A Lov- er sad, was part- ing from his dear one, And both were tast- ing bit- ter- ness and woe.
2. The years had quick- ly pass'd since they had part- ed, Thru' tri- als hard the youth had fought his way.

For tho' they long had planned up- on their mar- riage; Their par- ents both had stern- ly or- dered "No."
Tho' hin- dered oft, he main- tained his de- vo- tion, And per- se- vered nought else will ev- er pay.

"You are too young," they'd said, "and have no mon- ey," With which the fam- ily's bur- den to be- gin.
A lit- tle land he bought for a be- gin- ning, And quick- ly sold for dou- ble what he'd paid,

"Then let me go," he said, "and seek a for- tune, If I go West, I know I'm bound to win."
Thus pros- pered from the first, and blessed by Heav- en, The ground work for a for- tune soon was laid.

And thus had come a— bout the part—_____ ing, A time in— deed of sor— row and of fear,
The years of wait— ing fin— al— ly were ended. The day had come that seemed so far a— way.

But as he went he brave— ly did ad— dress her, And spoke, with love, these words of hope and cheer;
With wealth and hon— or crowned, with joy they mar— ried, And oft they thought of when he first did say:

**Chorus**

I will see you in Se— at— tle Ce—lia Mine, It won't be long till Nine—teen hun—dred nine. At the

Big A—las— kan Fair, When I've made my for—tune there, What a glad day that will be for both our lives, On the

shores of Pug–et Sound so fair to see, We'll be mar–ried at the splen–did A– Y– P, Life hence–

forth will all be song, Be it short or be it long, When I see you in Se–at–tle Ce–lia Mine.

*Panoramic view of the Alaska-Yukon-Pacific Exposition grounds, immortalized in*
*"I Will See You In Seattle, Celia Mine." Courtesy of Special Collections Division,*
*University of Washington Libraries.*

# Bow Down To Washington

Words and music by
Lester J. Wilson,
Class of 1913

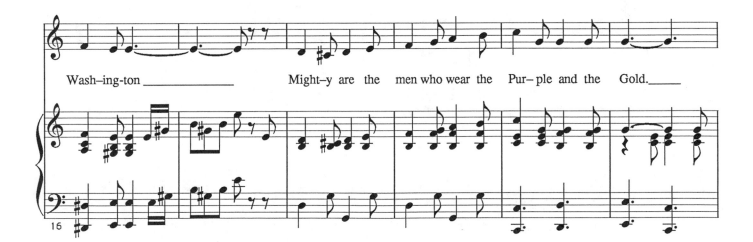

Bow down ____ to Wash–ing–ton _____ Bow down ____ to

Wash–ing–ton _____ Might–y are the men who wear the Pur–ple and the Gold. ____

75

hard-er to push them o–ver the line, than pass the Dar–dan–elles. ____ Vic– to– ry ! the cry of

Wash– ing– ton. ____ Leath-er lungs to–geth–er with a Rah ! Rah ! Rah ! And o'er ____ the

land ____ our joy– ous band will sing the glo-ry of Wash–ing–ton for– ev– er. er. ___

# The Cougar Fight Song

Words by Zella Melcher
Music by Phyllis Sayles
Class of 1919

78

Best in the West, we know you'll all do your best, So

on, on, on, on! Fight to the end!

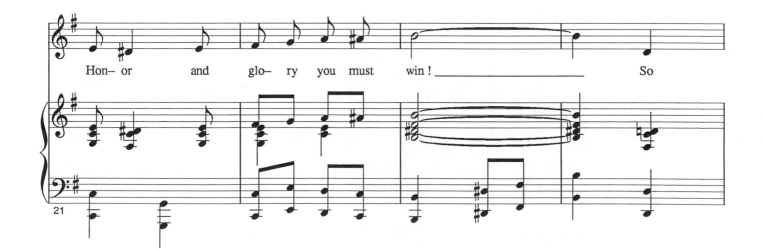

Hon- or and glo- ry you must win! _____ So

fight,     fight,     fight   for     Wash–ing–   ton   State   and

Vic–      to–      ry ! _____

*Pullman is the site of Washington's land grant university and its mascot, the cougar. Courtesy of Washington State University Library.*

# Cold Water

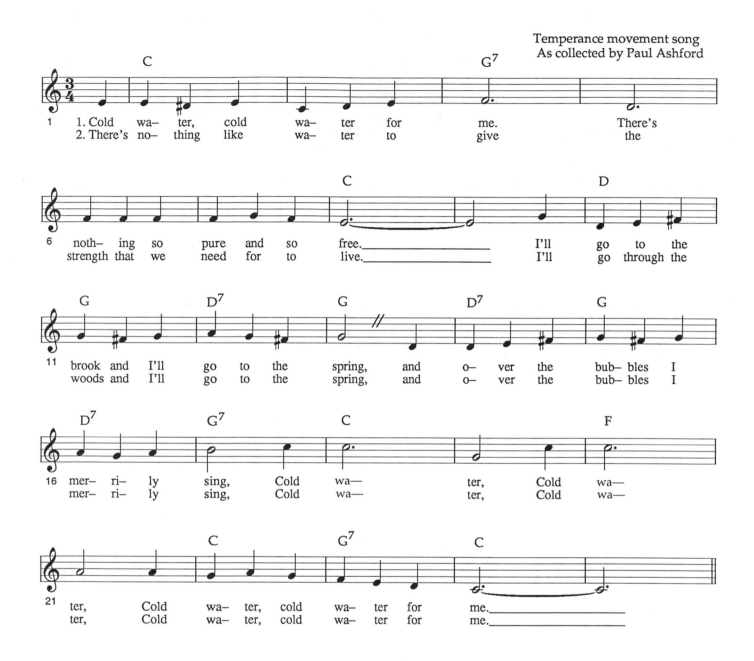

Temperance movement song
As collected by Paul Ashford

1. Cold wa— ter, cold wa— ter for me. There's noth— ing so pure and so free. I'll go to the brook and I'll go to the spring, and o— ver the bub— bles I mer— ri— ly sing, Cold wa— ter, Cold wa— ter, Cold wa— ter, cold wa— ter for me.

2. There's no— thing like wa— ter to give the strength that we need for to live. I'll go through the woods and I'll go to the spring, and o— ver the bub— bles I mer— ri— ly sing, Cold wa— ter, Cold wa— ter, Cold wa— ter, cold wa— ter for me.

81

# Shalom Aleichem

By Samuel and Israel Goldfarb

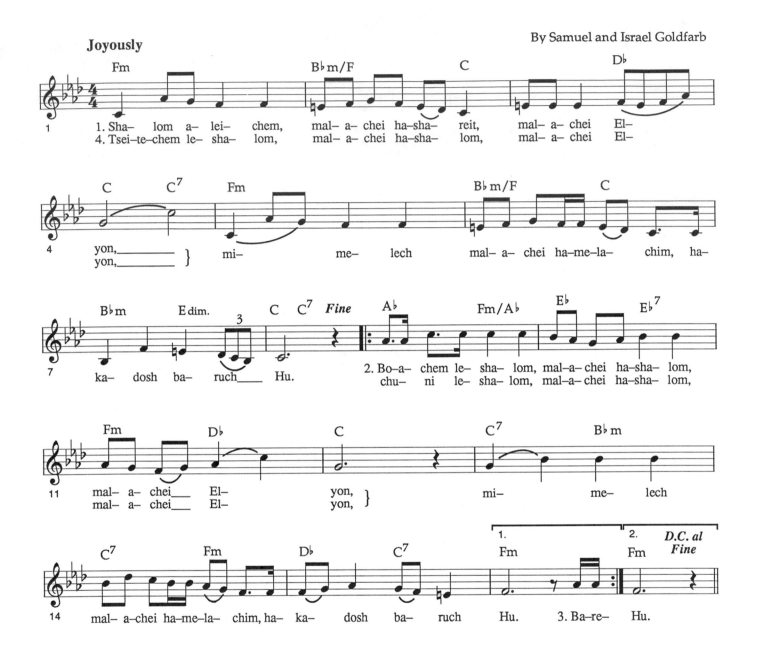

# Pop Songs from Washington

Washington State has produced many commercially successful singers and songwriters. In addition to others mentioned in this book, some familiar names who were born here, or who have lived and worked in Washington, include Heart (Ann and Nancy Wilson), Jimi Hendrix, Quincy Jones, Ray Charles, Diane Schuur, Robert Cray, Gail Davies, "Haywire Mac" McClintock, The Wailers, Loretta Lynn, and Carol Channing.

Perhaps the first Washington popular song composer to gain national attention was Charles Edward Bray, born in Philadelphia in 1844. Charles composed for many years in Portland, and his popularity spread to the Puget Sound area. In 1870 he was summoned to Seattle to prepare a local band for a grand Independence Day celebration. In 1886 Charles moved to Seattle to become orchestra director at Cordray's Theatre, a position he held through the early 1900s. Charles Bray's compositions have been carefully preserved by his granddaughter, Margaret Parcel of Seattle. **"One Smile For Me Sweetheart"** has a fresh and contemporary melody, with lyrics that reflect the sentimentality of the late 1800s and early 1900s.

The first national hit written and produced in the Northwest was **"Hindustan,"** published in 1918 by two Seattle songwriters, Oliver Wallace and Harold Weeks.

Oliver Wallace was known as the king of the silent picture show pipe organ players. During the 1920s he could be heard at the Liberty, the Dream, and the Coliseum theatres. He eventually moved to California to become a musical director at Walt Disney Studios, composing Donald Duck's Second World War hit "Der Fuhrer's Face" and scoring *Lady and the Tramp*.

Harold Weeks wrote some forty songs between 1910 and 1925, at the height of the songwriting craze before, during, and after the First World War. Weeks's last song, "Little Cabin In The Cascade Mountains," appears in chapter five. He ran The Melody Shop, the first popular song shop in Seattle, from 1917 to 1920. The shop was a center for musicians and composers—Seattle's own Tin Pan Alley. In a newspaper interview Weeks said, "The little shop was always packed with room for only thirteen customers at the counter. We had a piano on the balcony with windows opening to the street, and a dance band would sit up there and play and someone would sing through a megaphone as we demonstrated the songs the customers wanted to hear."

Mildred Chargois Tanner, who knew Harold Weeks when he was a hired hand on her parents'

*The cover of "Hindustan," a 1918 publication of The Melody Shop.*

farm near Ritzville, says that, "After working all day in the fields, he would rush to clean up and then dash into the house and to the piano, where in about 1912 he composed two of his most famous songs, 'Hindustan' and 'Dardanella.' "

Stoddard King was a columnist for the Spokane *Spokesman-Review* and a well-known lecturer and versifier. He wrote the words to **"There's A Long, Long Trail"** in 1914 while he was still a student at Yale. A schoolmate, Alonzo Elliot, wrote the melody. Turned down by American publishers, the song was published in England and was immediately taken up by the Tommies in Flanders, then by the Yanks as they moved into Argonne, and by the hundreds of thousands of soldiers that lay wounded on the battlefields and in the hospitals during the First World War. A 1917 newspaper account claimed the song was more popular than "It's A Long Way To Tipperary." The article went on to describe how the refrain rang from the throats of thousands of British soldiers as their transport *Tyndareus* sank off the coast of South Africa. Truly one of the most popular songs ever to come out of the Northwest, "There's A Long, Long Trail" remains a classic.

Stoddard King also published four books of verse and has become "the most plagiarized poet in the United States." His column for the *Spokesman-Review* reflected his quick wit, with quotes like the following from a 1929 "Facetious Fragments" column:

> *The St. Louis authorities have put a stop to children's flagpole sitting contests, on the ground that such nonstop roosting is bad for the health of the little ones. But what of the parents? Have they no rights? If little Junior is sitting on a flagpole, father and mother know where he is every minute of the time. And that is no small boon.*
>
> *One child and one flagpole would prove all that science needs to know, namely, whether it is possible for an adolescent to sit in one spot for more than five minutes at a time.*

Certainly no book about Washington's

*The cover of "Black Ball Ferry Line," 1951.*

music would be complete without a mention of the state's most famous all-around entertainer—Bing Crosby.

Harry Lillis Crosby was born on May 2, 1901, the fourth of seven children. His grandfather, a sea captain named Nathaniel Crosby, was a founding father of Olympia. Harry was born in Tacoma, baptized in St. Patrick's Church, and lived his first years on North Jay Street. The family later moved to Spokane, where a neighbor boy gave Harry the nickname "Bing," after a big-eared cartoon character. The family's modest income allowed for few luxuries, so Bing earned spending money by picking apples, working as a lumberjack, and covering a paper route for the *Spokesman-Review*. He attended Webster Grade School and Gonzaga High School.

In 1920 he entered Gonzaga University to study law, but soon gave it up for singing and drumming with a band called the Musicaladers. In 1925 Bing and piano player Al Rinker left Spokane in a battered Model-T Ford. After three weeks on the road, a hundred punctures and blowouts and dozens of parts replaced, the car died eighty miles short of Hollywood. Stranded and broke, the pair finally limped into Hollywood to stay with Al's sister, jazz singer Mildred Bailey. Thus began a journey into the heart and soul of America for one of this country's most beloved performers.

"**Black Ball Ferry Line**" was recorded by Bing and the Andrews Sisters in 1951, as well as by Percy Faith and his orchestra. There were numerous performances of the song on radio shows of the early 1950s by such singers as Edgar Bergen and Charlie McCarthy. As well as being performed by a Washingtonian, "Black Ball Ferry Line" was written by two former Washingtonians. John Rarig, born and raised in Seattle, worked for thirty-five years in the Los Angeles area as an arranger, singer, and pianist. Dixie Lou Thompson was born in Kent, and worked in Los Angeles as a script consultant and production assistant for radio and television.

The Fleetwoods—Gretchen Christopher, Gary Troxel, and Barbara Ellis—were students at Olympia High School when they recorded the first gold record produced in Washington State: "**Come Softly To Me.**" The song reached number one on *Billboard's* charts nationally in March 1959. The group, which had only performed publicly twice before recording the song, appeared on "The Ed Sullivan Show," and soon saw fifteen singles make it onto the *Billboard* charts. Their hits included "Mr. Blue," also a number one song in 1959, "Tragedy," and "Runaround." The group's name was taken from Olympia's telephone exchange. Gretchen Christopher, composer of "Come Softly To Me," still lives and performs in Olympia.

Perhaps the most enduring Northwest folk group to come out of the "folk boom"of the 1960s was The Brothers Four. The Brothers Four began in 1958, when University of Washington fraternity brothers Bob Flick, Mike Kirkland, John Paine, and Dick Foley formed the group and had such hits as "Green Leaves Of Summer," "Try To Remember," and their greatest hit, "**Green Fields.**" The version of the song recorded by The Brothers Four was written by Terry Gilkyson and The Easy Riders.

However, Bob Flick has said that there is a much older version of the tune that was a favorite of Abraham Lincoln.

The song "**Seattle,**" which was recorded by Perry Como in 1968, gained its popularity as the theme song for the television series "Here Come the Brides." The series was loosely based on the fact that during the 1860s Asa Mercer brought about one hundred women to Seattle to provide wives for the mostly male settlers. All but one

*The cover of "Seattle," the theme song for "Here Come the Brides."*

did marry local men. These women have come to be known as "Mercer Girls."

The popular songs included in this chapter range from the romantic "heart" songs of the turn of the century to the mellow music of Bing Crosby. They're songs with a uniquely Northwest connection—they are about Washington, composed here, or written or recorded by Washington musicians. Find a favorite of yours and sing along!

# One Smile For Me Sweetheart

Words and music by
Charles E. Bray

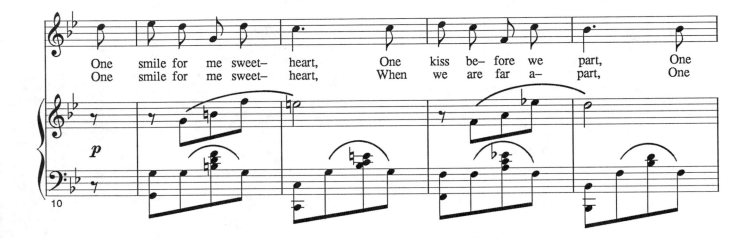

One smile for me sweet—heart, One kiss be—fore we part, One
One smile for me sweet—heart, When we are far a—part, One

fond and sweet ca—ress, One lit—tle gol—den tress, One
prayer for my re—turn, When Heaven's night tor—ches burn, One

Public domain

loving thought of me, When I am far from thee, One
home for thee and me, By love's sweet labor won, One

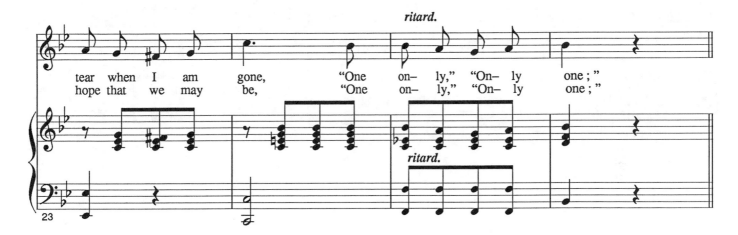

tear when I am gone, "One only," "Only one;"
hope that we may be, "One only," "Only one;"

**Chorus**

*Sop.* "One only" "Only one" One smile for me sweetheart; One fond and sweet ca-

*Alto*

*Ten.* "One only" "Only one" One smile for me sweetheart; One fond and sweet ca-

*Bass*

ress,     One  lit–tle  gol–den  tress,     One  tear  when I am  gone,     "One    on–ly,"  "On–ly    one."

*ritenuto*

ress,     One  lit–tle  gol–den  tress,     One  tear  when I am  gone,     "One    on–ly,"  "On–ly    one."

*ritenuto et dim.*

8

# Hindustan

By Oliver G. Wallace
and Harold Weeks

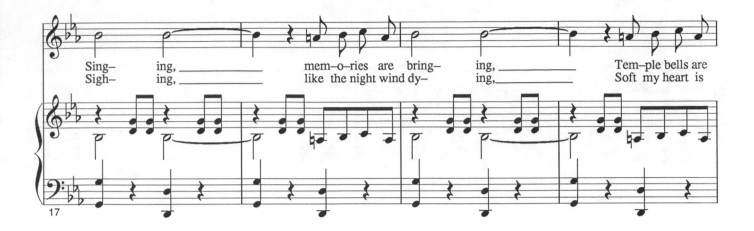

Sing— ing, _____ mem—o—ries are bring— ing, _____ Tem—ple bells are
Sigh— ing, _____ like the night wind dy— ing,_____ Soft my heart is

ring— ing, _____ Call-ing me a— far. _____
cry— ing, _____ for my love a— far. _____

**Chorus**

Hin— — du — stan, _____ where we stopped to rest our tired__ car— a—

van, _____ Hin — — du— stan, _____ Where the paint–ed pea-cock

proud–ly spreads his fan, _____ Hin — — du— stan, _____ where the

pur—ple sun–bird flashed a–cross the sand, _____ Hin — — du— stan, _____

where I met her and the world be— gan. _____ gan. _____

# There's A Long, Long Trail

Words by Stoddard King
Music by Zo Elliot

Nights are grow-ing ver-y lone— ly, Days are ver-y long;____
All night long I hear you call— ing, Call— ing sweet and low;____

I'm a-grow-ing wear-y on— ly, List— 'ning for your song.____
Seem to hear your foot-steps fall— ing, Ev— 'ry— where I go.____

93

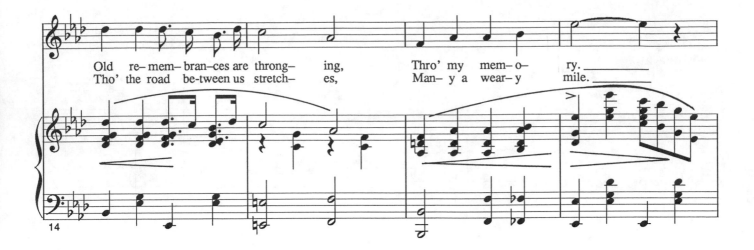

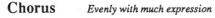

night- in-gales are sing-ing, And a white moon beams: ___ There's a

long, long night of wait-ing___ Un-til my dreams all come true; ___ Till the

day when I'll be go-ing down that long, long trail with you. There's a you. ___

1.

2.

## Marching Chorus

**In Martial Time** *(But not fast)*

There's a long, long trail a wind–ing ____ In–to the land of ____ my dreams, ____

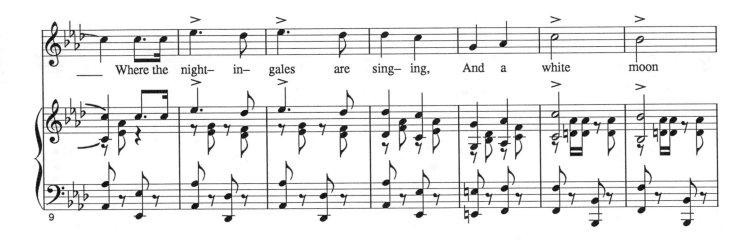

____ Where the night– in– gales are sing– ing, And a white moon

beams : ____ There's a long, long night of wait– ing, ____ Un– til my dreams all ____

_\_\_\_ come true; \_\_\_\_\_ Till the day when I'll be go— ing down that_

_long, long trail with you. There's a you._

# Black Ball Ferry Line

By Dixie Lou Thompson
and John Rarig

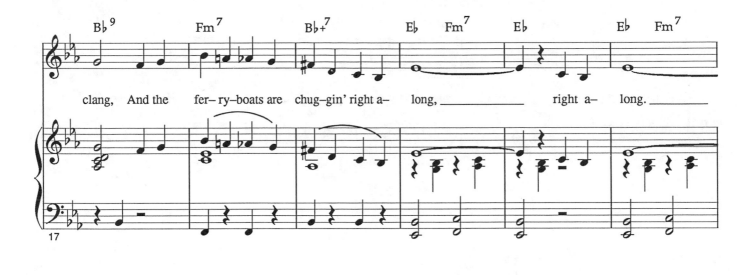

clang, And the fer–ry–boats are chug–gin' right a– long, _____ right a– long. _____

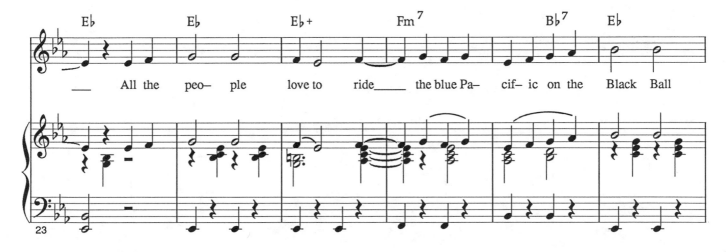

All the peo– ple love to ride_____ the blue Pa– cif– ic on the Black Ball

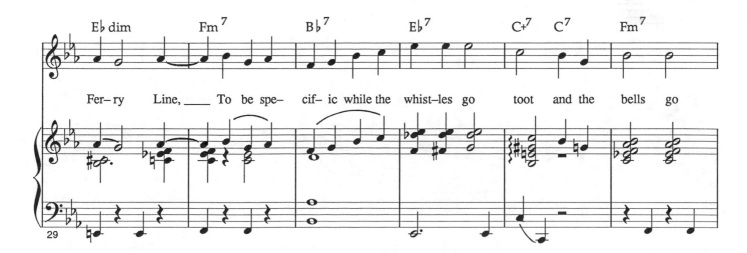

Fer– ry Line, _____ To be spe– cif– ic while the whist–les go toot and the bells go

clang, And the fer–ry–boats are chug–gin' right a– long,_____ right a– long.

Up on the up– per deck____ the view is great by heck,___ You love your gal a peck
Down in the en– gine room____ the boil–ers hum a tune,___ They're sing–in' love in bloom

__ and you're in clov–er. And when the whist– les blow____ you hate to go be– low_
__ with deep e– mo– tion. And on the deck a– bove____ each hap–py pair in love_

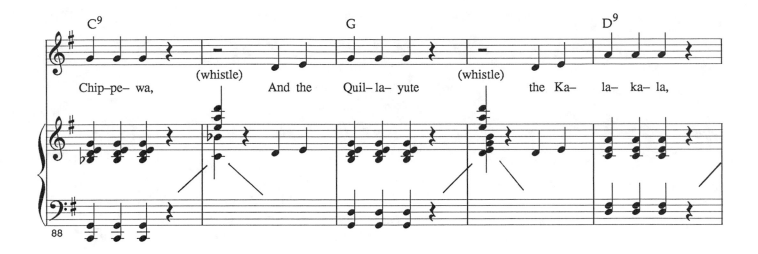

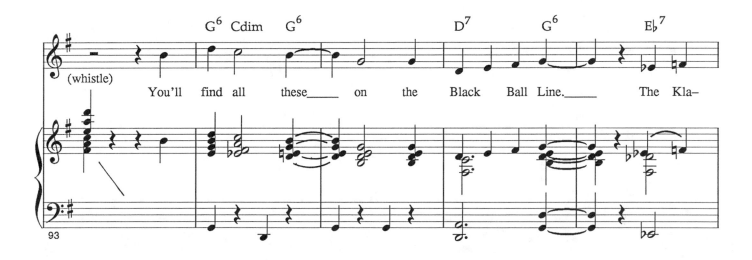

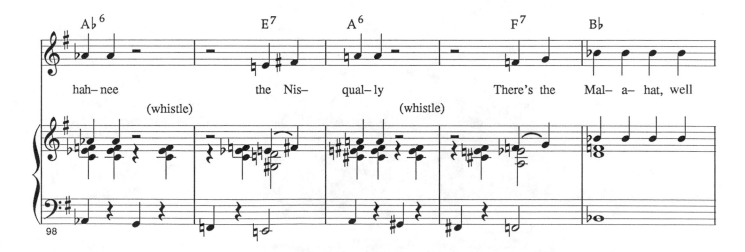

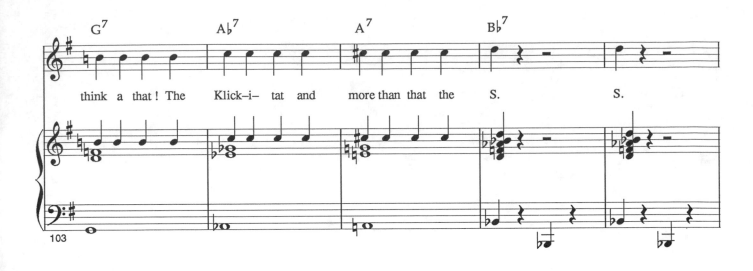

think a that! The Klick–i– tat and more than that the S. S.

D. S. al Fine 𝄋

Cit–y of Sac– ra– men– to. On the

*The* SS Leschi *on Puget Sound, 1931, twenty years before Bing Crosby and the Andrews Sisters recorded "Black Ball Ferry Line." Courtesy of Museum of History and Industry.*

# Come Softly To Me

By Gary Troxel,
Gretchen Christopher
and Barbara Ellis

Come soft–ly, dar–ling. Come soft–ly, dar–ling, come to me

stay ___ You're my ob– ses–sion for– ev– er and a day. ___

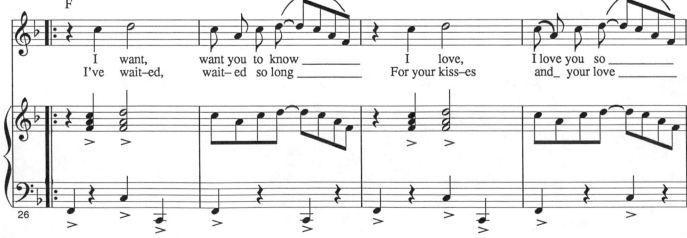

I want, want you to know _____ I love, I love you so _____
I've wait–ed, wait–ed so long _____ For your kiss–es and_ your love _____

# Green Fields

Words and music by Terry Gilkyson,
Rick Dehr and Frank Miller

How can I keep search–ing when dark clouds hide the day? I on–ly know there's

noth–ing here for me, Noth–ing in this wide world left for me to see. But

I'll ____ keep on wait–ing 'til ____ you re–turn, I'll ____ keep on wait–ing un–

til the day you learn, You can't be hap–py while your heart's on the roam.

You can't be hap–py un– til you bring it home, Home ____ to the green fields and

me once a– gain. _____

# Seattle

Words and music by
Hugo Montenegro, Jack Keller
and Ernie Sheldon

**Moderately**

**Chorus**

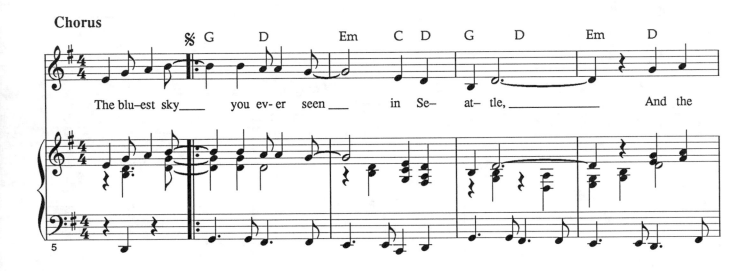

The blu–est sky___ you ev- er seen ___ in Se– at– tle, _____ And the

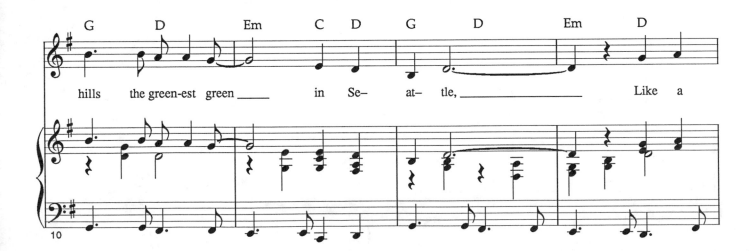

hills the green–est green _____ in Se– at– tle, _____ Like a

beau– ti–ful child _____ grow– ing up free and wild, _____ Full of

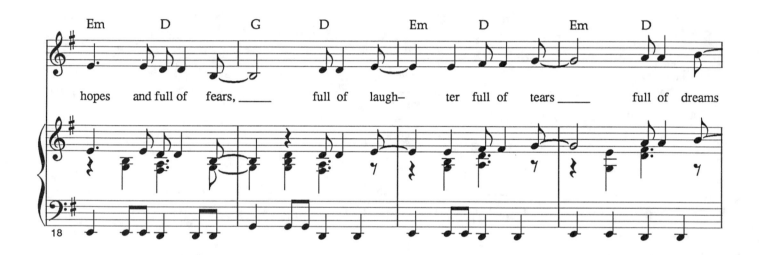

hopes and full of fears, _____ full of laugh– ter full of tears _____ full of dreams

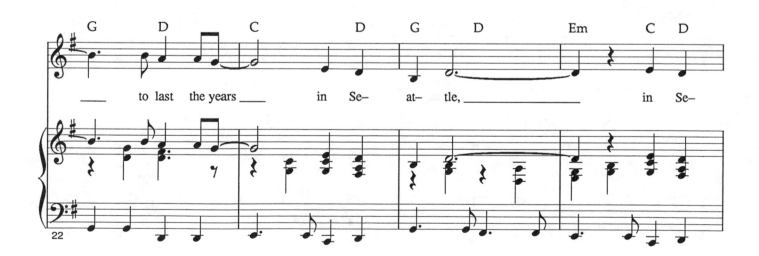

_____ to last the years _____ in Se– at– tle, _____ in Se–

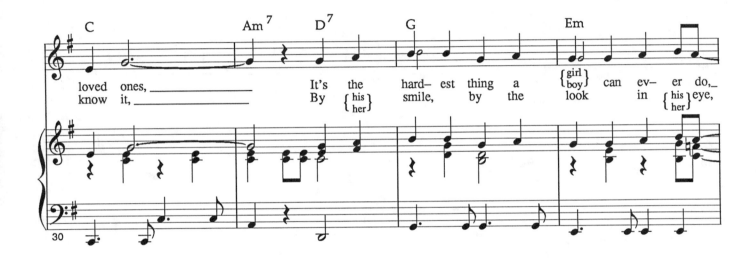

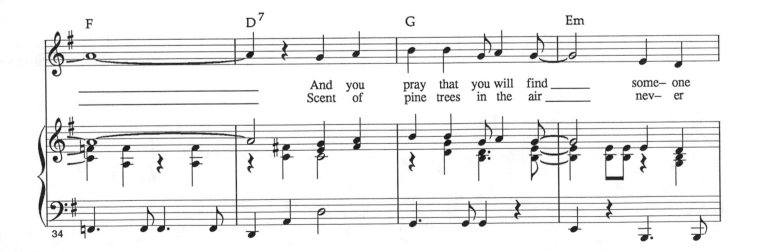

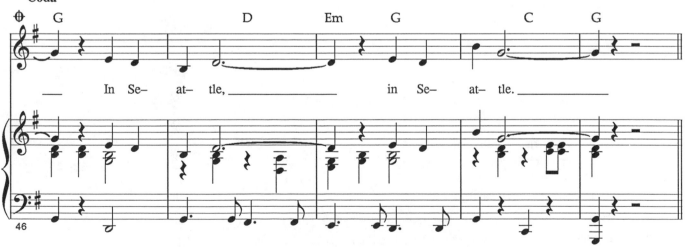

3.  If you ever fall in love with a logger,
    There is something you will have to understand,
    For as much as he may care you will always have
        to share,
    His love with his green mountain land.

*CHORUS*

115

# Passing of the Old Ways

The only certainty in life is change—a passing of the old ways. In this chapter the cost of progress is examined. From the 1894 version of "The Old Settler" to "Our State Is A Dumpsite," these thoughtful songs contain valuable lessons.

Judge Francis Henry, author of "The Old Settler" (see chapter one), lamented the rapid changes he witnessed in Washington's early days, and he wrote a 1904 sequel to his popular song. Present-day environmental activists will find that the theme of the second part of "The Old Settler" sounds quite familiar.

Some say that this country's improving,
And boast of its commerce and trade;
But measured by social enjoyment,
I find it has sadly decayed.

In the pioneer days on the Sound,
When people had little to wear,
And subsisted on clams the year round,
We'd hearty good fellowship here.

The thoughtful, industrious old settler,
Was so fond of obliging a friend,
That if anyone wanted his tools,
He'd always quit working to lend.

At our gatherings for pastoral pleasure,
Dance, picnic, or social knockdown,
One man was as good as another,
No kind of distinction was shown.

But now when I go to a party,
The people around me seem froze;
They dare not to be social and hearty,
For fear they may soil their store clothes.

Not only our friendly relations,
Are dropped for the worship of gold,
But the solid backbone of the country,
Is recklessly bargained and sold.

They're slashing and selling our timber,
Not taking the slightest concern,
For what we shall do in the future,
Without any stovewood to burn.

They're wasting the natural resources,
Our bountiful waters contain;
They're canning our clams and our oysters,
And shipping them off for more gain.

And even the climate is changing,
For only some ten years ago,
Strawberries got ripe in December,
Whilst now it brings four feet of snow.
  —*Reminiscences of Washington
      Territory
    By Charles Prosch*

*My people are few. They resemble the scattering trees of a storm-swept plain . . . There was a time when our people covered the land as waves of a wind-ruffled sea cover its shell-paved floor, but that time long since passed away with the greatness of tribes that are now but a mournful memory. . . .*

*When the last Red Man shall have perished, and the memory of my tribe*

*Drawing of the Hillaire family by Robert Aiston. Courtesy of Rich and Lylene Johnson.*

*shall have become a myth among the white man, these shores will swarm with the invisible dead of my tribe, and when your children's children think themselves alone in the field, the shore, the shop, or in the silence of the pathless woods, they will not be alone . . . At night when the streets of your cities and villages are silent and you think them deserted, they will throng with the returning hosts that once filled them and still love this beautiful land. The White Man will never be alone.*

*Let him be just and deal kindly with my people, for the dead are not powerless. Dead—I say? There is no death. Only a change of worlds.*

*—Chief Seattle*
*Spoken to Governor Isaac Stevens at the signing of the Port Elliott Treaty, in which Chief Seattle surrendered the land upon which the city of Seattle is now located*

Twilo Scofield wrote **"As Long As The Grass Shall Grow"** in 1977 after reading *Touch the Earth* by T. C. McLuhan. The book contains speeches given by Native American tribal leaders. The verses are paraphrased from speeches given by Nez Perce Chief Joseph, Red Jacket of the Seneca, Ten Bears of the Comanche, Seattle of the Duwamish, and Dan George, hereditary chief of the Coast Salish, among others.

**"Do Not Mortgage The Farm"** appeared in editions of *Grange Melodies* published between 1891 and 1925. The song came from the epidemic of farm foreclosures that occurred from the 1870s to the 1890s. Farm foreclosures are again a reality; the accompanying human tragedy and loss of irreplaceable skills make this song timely once again.

Whaling was once an active industry in Washington. The Bay City whaling station operated from 1911 to 1925 near Aberdeen and "processed" gray, humpback, fin, sperm, sei, blue, and bottlenose whales. In 1916, 334 whales were killed and 14,160 barrels of whale oil were recorded. Whaling in Washington declined after the First World War due to a decline in the demand for whale products—and in the number of whales.

*Despite our much-vaunted ability to probe the secrets of the universe, we have so far failed to probe the mystery of the mind of the whale. If we are to make amends to the whale nation for the despicable savagery with which we have treated their members in the past, we must do so now. In a few more years there will be nothing left that we can do for them . . . except write their epitaph.*
*—Farley Mowat*
  *A Whale For Killing*

*Orca. Courtesy of Heimlich-Boran/The Whale Museum.*

Linda Waterfall wrote **"The Whale Song"** after performing at a benefit concert for Friday Harbor's Whale Museum. The song expresses the current public awareness of the plight of the whale.

*Some of the museum staff took me out in a boat. . . and we were lucky enough to observe a pod of Orca whales. I never felt afraid, even though we were surrounded by these powerful creatures, and one even breached quite near the boat. From their peaceful aura, and from the information I learned about their singing and their behavior, I imagine them to be highly intelligent, evolved creatures, perhaps more so than we humans.*

*—Linda Waterfall*

When Hanford, Washington, was identified as a likely site to receive over half of the nation's radioactive nuclear waste by the beginning of the twenty-first century, Dana Lyons voiced his protest in the song **"Our State Is A Dumpsite."** The Washington Public Interest Research Group (WashPIRG) adopted "Our State Is A Dumpsite" as the theme song for its "Don't Sacrifice Washington" campaign. They also lobbied for the song to be recognized as the state song for Washington. Representative Dean Sutherland points out:

*. . . much of the nation still perceives us as being eager to take radioactive waste. This song sends a message from our state to the rest of the nation: Washington is very concerned about the storage of nuclear waste. Future generations will want to know what we were concerned about. This song deserves to be in the book* [Washington Songs and Lore] *so they will know more of what was being said about the nuclear waste problem.*

*The "Shoshone Flyer." Courtesy of Washington State Historical Society.*

. . . Old 7's days are over now,
She won't come back no more,
The railroad track don't shake and jump
Like it used to do before;
They've made a brand new truck road—
Where the railroad ran before,
And C. Z. Kenworths haul the logs
Down to Deep River's shore.
You can listen for the whistle
When she rounds Hendrickson's place,
And the 'ding-dong' at the crossing—
As she nears the log dump 'race'
You can listen for the brake squeal
And the 'ding-dongs' of yore,
But those treasured sounds are silent—
She just won't 'ding-dong' no more.

    *—From "Old No. 7"*
     *By Woody Gifford*

Yes, with progress comes change. Gil Dickson's lament for the passing of an era is a fitting closure to this selection of songs that remind us that change is not always for the better.

Now they've taken away the railroad,
But my memories linger on,
No more trains will be coming,
It's a sad thing they have done.
It makes me feel so lonely,
Not to hear the whistle scream,
They've taken up the railroad tracks,
And it's taken my childhood dreams.

    *—From "The Railroad Is Gone"*
     *By Gil Dickson*

# As Long As The Grass Shall Grow

Words and music by
Twilo Scofield

119

As long as the moon will rise,_____ And as

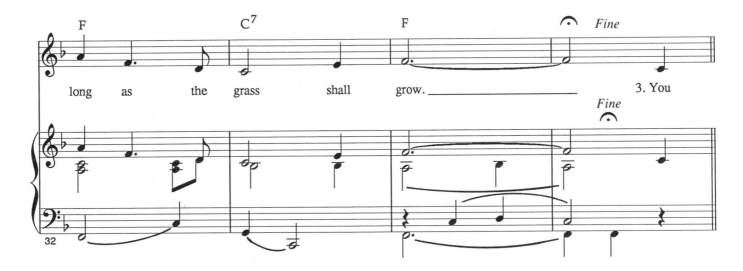

long as the grass shall grow._____ 3. You

*Fine*

---

*Fine*

CHORUS

3. You lit our lodges for your campfires,
   In the ashes left dust and blood.
   We thought half our land would satisfy you,
   But we found out that it never would.

CHORUS

4. You left us like birds with broken wings,
   All scattered like stones on the ground.
   But in silent fields and pathless woods,
   Our dreams and our spirits are found.

CHORUS

5. For we have known when the forests were free,
   And the wind spirits roamed our land.
   And everything that was needed for life,
   We took with a gentle hand.

CHORUS

6. The sky is round and the earth is round,
   And the sun and the stars and the moon.
   The seasons all move in a circle too,
   And our spring will come again soon.

# Do Not Mortgage The Farm

By E. R. Latta and
James L. Orr

1. For–tune may some–times for– sake you,   Use– less the strug-gle may   seem ; _____
2. Think of the time it  has tak– en,   Think of the toil it  has   cost, _____   That

But   be not tempt-ed to   haz– ard, ____   That which you may not re–   deem ; _____
you  and your child-ren might   own it, ____   Now  do  not let it be   lost ; _____

Do    not im–per–il   the   home–stead, ____   Ban– ish the thought in a–   larm, _____
Think  of the hearts that en–   shrine you, ____   And trust you to   shield them from harm, _____

122

Make it your strong res—o— lu— tion, Nev— er to mort-gage the farm. _____

Do not mort-gage, not mort-gage the farm, Do not mort-gage, not mort-gage the farm; For

Do not mort-gage the farm, _____ Do not mort-gage the farm; _____ For

sor— row will soon o—ver— take you, _____ If ev— er you mort-gage the farm. _____

sor— row will soon o—ver— take you, _____ If ev— er you mort-gage the farm. _____

3.     If you would peacefully slumber,
Knowing no waking regret,
See that your right to the homestead,
Is not encumbered by debt;
Strictest economy practice,
And toil with a vigorous arm,
Make it your strong resolution,
Never to mortgage the farm.

# The Whale Song

Words and music by
Linda Waterfall

**Slowly and smoothly**

1. Once we were dream-ing of a wa-ter-y world, Un-der the surf and the mir-ror of the sky_
2. Deep in the wa- ter is the way that we dream, Sleep-ing it seems but real-ly we are lis—ten_

_ ing, and we ____ won- dered why we had to walk on earth,
_ ing, to the voice of this dream, That's how we learn to sing,

124

Years and years and years go by ___ Chang—ing is so slow;
Si— lent in the dark— ness now, The voice will show you where;

Won— d'ring if you've moved at all, you hard-ly ev— er know, ___
You must have great faith in it, It is ___ al— ways there, ___

Now I re- mem- ber as I'm swim-ming a— way, A rum-or they say that once we walked on
Deep in the wa- ter and the sing-ing we share, Ris-ing for air, and the hea-vens that greet our

land,
eyes,

I know we nev-er will a— gain.
We're ver- y glad to be a— live.

gain.

Peace,___

_____ friend. _____

3.    Once I was singing and I heard your song.
I followed you along—
Your voice is of the water
Still you kill my brother,
But I think I understand.
I know what is hurting you—
You have lost your faith,
When your children cry in fear,
You don't know what to say.
Maybe someday you'll believe again,
You are our friend,
In the One that never ends—
Maybe you'll never kill again.
Peace, friend.

# Our State Is A Dumpsite

Words and music by
Dana Lyons

1. I lost my job here fish— in' and o— pened up a store, I
2. We don't just make the pow— er, we al— so build the bombs, The

buy and sell re— ac— tors, cool— ing tow— ers, and lead doors ; We've
dol— lars ne— ver stop from Wash— ing— ton to Wash— ing— ton ; The

got a brand new in— dus— try bear— ing fruit of fin— er taste, We sell
oth— er states all love us 'cause we rare— ly take a stand, They

juice to Cal— i— for— nia and get paid to keep the waste.
send us lit— tle pres— ents and put mon— ey in our hands.

**Chorus**

Our state is a dump— site, plu— ton— i— um two— thir— ty— nine,

Our state is a dump— site, just set it o— ver there that's fine !

127

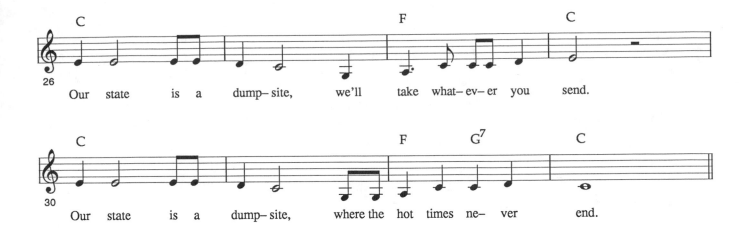

Our state is a dump–site, we'll take what–ev–er you send.

Our state is a dump–site, where the hot times ne–ver end.

---

3. So now I'm fat and wealthy 'cause my business
          here has grown,
   I sell lamps that don't plug in and heaters for your
          home.
   Progress and technology, for us they've sure been
          great
   We're singing here in Washington, the
          ever-glowing state.

*FINAL CHORUS*

*Our state is a dumpsite, plutonium 239,*
*Our state is a dumpsite, just set it over there that's*
          *fine!*
*Our state is a dumpsite, our fate is to mutate*
*We're singing here in Washington, the ever-glowing*
          *state.*

*FINAL CHORUS*

*CHORUS*

# Washington, My Home

This chapter contains a collection of Washington's "state songs"—proposed and official. The fact that it takes an entire chapter to hold just some of these special songs is evidence that Washingtonians really care about their "state song."

One of the earliest songs considered the state song was "The Old Settler" (see chapter one). *The People's Song Bulletin* mentions that a Washingtonian wrote in to say that "Acres Of Clams" used to be the state song, until some of the newer settlers thought it too undignified!

"Washington, Beloved" was written by highly esteemed professor and former legislator Edmond S. Meany in collaboration with musician Reginald DeKoven, for a 1909 collection of university songs, *The Washington Song-Book*. Despite passage that year of legislation declaring the song to be the state anthem of Washington, it never caught on. Still, as late as 1935 copies were being distributed to school children by the secretary of state. Harry Bauer, in an article entitled "Requiem for an Anthem" (*Pacific Northwest Quarterly*), wrote:

> *It is highly questionable whether legislators are well advised in usurping the traditional prerogative of citizens by arbitrarily adopting a state song. In questions relating to the fine arts, a legislature should confirm, not affirm . . . The few state songs that are well known were accepted and beloved by the people long before the respective legislatures confirmed the fact by official ratification.*

In the minds of many Washingtonians, **"Hail Washington"** by Rose Cole Boettiger was considered to be the state song from around 1911 until 1959, when "Washington, My Home" was selected by the legislature as the state song. Although "Hail Washington" was proclaimed the state song on sheet music published in 1925,

its real status came from the esteem in which it was held by Washington residents. In a 1962 letter to Governor Rosellini, a writer bemoaned the replacement of the "real Washington song" she had sung in grade school in 1919. The governor's response indicated that he, also, "remembered the old song well." Even recently, a number of letters came to the Centennial Commission with recollections of "Hail Washington" learned in childhood. It was particularly impressive that, over fifty years later, people could still remember all the words.

Another song popular during the 1940s, **"It's A Hundred To One You're From Washington,"** was written by Al Hoffman around 1938. Hoffman came to the United States from Minsk, Russia, in 1908. He demonstrated an interest in music early in life, and for a time led a band in Seattle. In 1928 Hoffman moved to New York and began writing songs that firmly

*Seattle's Orpheum featuring Al Hoffman, Composer. Courtesy of Special Collections Division, University of Washington Libraries.*

established him as one of the leading composers to come from Washington. A few of his hits, usually written in collaboration with other composers and lyricists, include "Fit As A Fiddle," 1932; "Mairzy Doats," 1944; "If I Knew You Were Comin' I'd've Baked A Cake,"1950; and "Hawaiian Wedding Song," 1958.

Helen Davis, of South Bend, wrote the current official Washington State song, **"Washington, My Home,"** in 1952 for the dedication of Fort Columbia as a national monument. The song was arranged by Stuart Churchill and was adopted by the legislature in 1959. Helen herself was referred to by Don Duncan of the *Seattle Times* as "one of the home-grown delights who keep the Pacific Northwest from being dull." Another of her works, "Wet Me Down In Washington," appears in chapter four.

A bill was passed in the 1987 legislature making **"Roll On, Columbia"** the state's official folk song. This popular folk song about Washington was written in 1941 by Woody Guthrie when Guthrie worked for the Bonneville Power Administration. The coming of the dams was not without impact. Native Americans lament the loss of traditional fishing grounds at Kettle Falls and the great changes that were brought about in their lives.

*I saw the Columbia River and the big Grand Coulee Dam from just about every cliff, mountain, tree, and post from which it can be seen. I made up twenty-six songs about the Columbia and about the dam and about the men, and these songs were recorded by the Department of Interior, Bonneville Power Administration out in Portland. The records were played at all sorts and sizes of meetings where people bought bonds to bring the power lines over the fields and hills to their own little places. Electricity to milk the cows, kiss the maid, shoe the old mare, light up the saloon, the chili joint window, the schools, and churches along the way, to run the factories turning out manganese, chrome, bauxite, aluminum and steel.*

—Woody Guthrie
*California to the New York Island*

But that's not the end of the state song story. It all began in early 1985, when Seattle comedian Ross Shafer suggested on his "Almost Live" television show that "Louie, Louie," by Richard Berry of Los Angeles, should be Washington's state song. Craig Cole, a councilman in Whatcom County, picked up on

*Cartoon by Brian Basset. Copyright © 1985 The Seattle Times.*
*Used by permission. All rights reserved.*

the idea and managed to push a resolution through the county council urging the legislature to make "Louie, Louie" the official state song, and to name the next county Louie, Louie County. Governor Booth Gardner, who was urged to take a stand on the issue, did proclaim April twelfth "Louie, Louie Day." The legislature was subjected to intense lobbying from Washington baby boomers, many of whom considered "Louie, Louie" their anthem.

In the midst of the movement to install "Louie, Louie" as the state song, Erik Lacitis of the *Seattle Times* contacted Richard Berry. Berry wrote a Washington State version of the lyrics, inspired by a train ride into Washington for a "Louie, Louie" reunion held in Tacoma. To quote Richard Berry: "Every time I think nothing more can happen with this song, something does . . . There's just something magical about this song."

Cover of the official state song. Courtesy of Department of Commerce and Economic Development, State of Washington.

Ultimately, "Washington, My Home" retained its status as Washington's state song. However, a compromise measure has been proposed to name "Louie, Louie" as the official rock song of Washington, with Richard Berry's Washington lyrics. We were unable to obtain permission to print the Washington lyrics to "Louie, Louie"—but no one knows the words to the original version, either!

Why "Louie, Louie" as a state song? To quote Ross Shafer:

> We think 'Louie, Louie' is an appropriate state song because it's easy to dance to. We tried to dance to 'Washington, My Home,' but it's awkward, in between a waltz and a polka. But 'Louie, Louie' can be danced to by all the classic dances, from the Bump to the Chicken.

Suggestions to replace "Washington, My Home" with either "Louie, Louie" or "Roll On, Columbia" opened the door to a flood of support and opposition, and countless new offerings of Washington songs. Thomas "Red" Kelly, one of the founding fathers and gubernatorial candidate of the infamous OWL party of the 1976 election and a well-regarded musician, wrote **"Our State Of Washington"** as his submission for the state song of Washington.

> With all the interest and frivolity involved in the OWL Party, I wanted to point out that along with the fun and games—when the score is tallied, I love my home very much . . . Having lived here longer than any place in my previously restless life, my roots embrace not only the land, lush and green, scenery unmatched, but also so many people (OWLs or not) with the vitality and warmth that give the crown its jewels. All these riches in my life urge me to try to put something in the melting pot! I wrote the song to say 'THANK YOU' to God—and every one who lives here.
>
> —Thomas "Red" Kelly

A state song is more than an official statement about the residents. The songs in this chapter reflect loyalty, pride, and a sense of humor about the place Washingtonians call home. A serious song? A rock n' roll song? A folk song? A comical song? It's up to you, the singers.

# Hail Washington

Words and music by
Rose Cole Boettiger

Wash–ing–ton we love you just be–cause you're what you are, _____ Tho'
Wash–ing–ton you thrill us with your firs and ce–dars high, _____ Like

we may trav—el near, _____ Tho' we may trav—el far. _____ There's
sen—tin—els stand by, _____ Point—ing to the sky. _____ Your

**F**

some—thing grand a—bout you makes our hearts beat fond and true, _____ For
moun—tain streams en—chant us as they gai—ly wend their way, _____ Our

**C7**

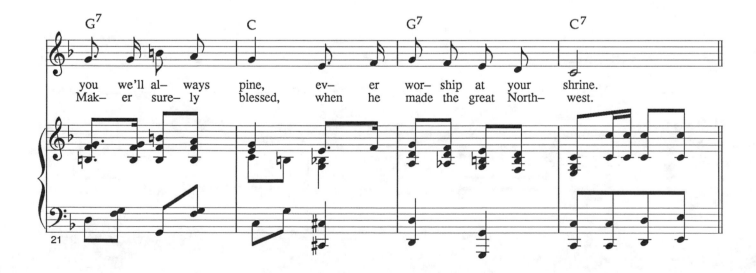

you we'll al—ways pine, ev—er wor—ship at your shrine.
Mak—er sure—ly blessed, when he made the great North—west.

**G7** **C** **G7** **C7**

**Chorus**

Hail to our Wash–ing–ton, _____ Our

Wash– ing– ton, _____ Where the lakes and moun–tains so ma–

jes– tic, _____ Glo– ri– fy the set– ting sun, _____

Grain fields lend splen– dor, _____ or– chard

blos– soms sweet–ly scent the air; _____ 'Tis the State that's ev– er

green, May it al– ways reign su– preme, Wash — ing —

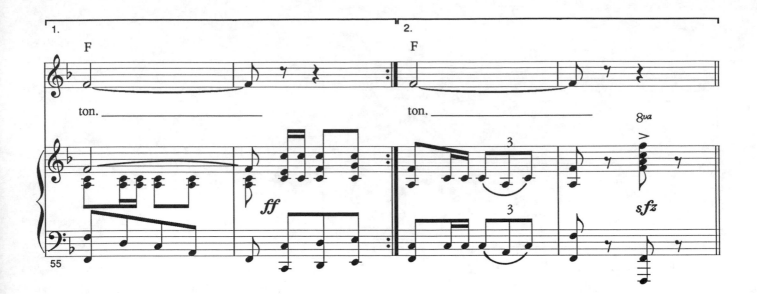

# Washington, My Home

Words and music by
Helen Davis
Arranged by Stuart Churchill

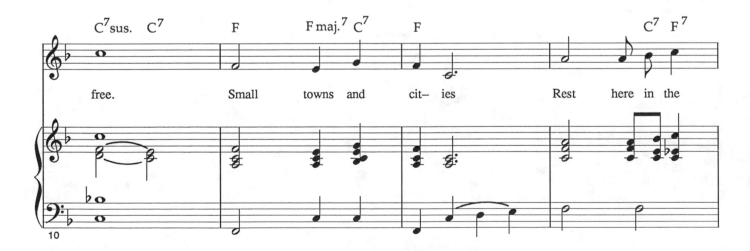

mf This is my coun—try; God gave it to me; I will pro—tect it, Ev—er keep it free. Small towns and cit—ies Rest here in the

137

sun, Filled with our laugh-ter. Thy will be done.

**Refrain**

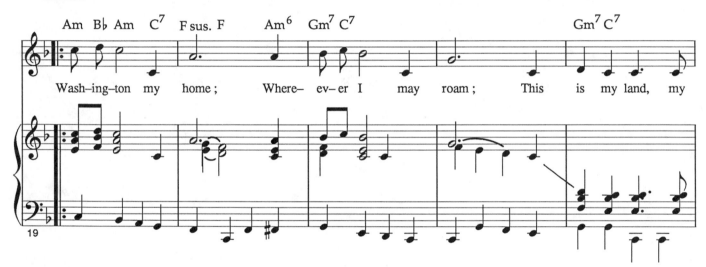

Wash-ing-ton my home; Where—ev-er I may roam; This is my land, my

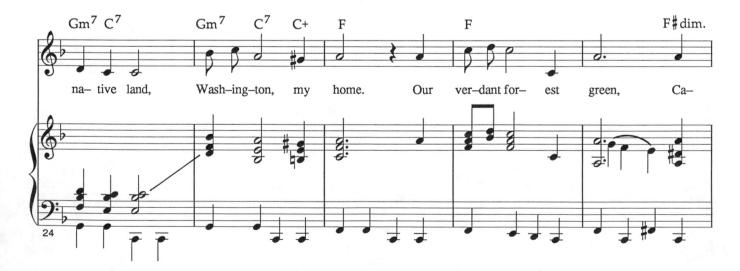

na—tive land, Wash-ing-ton, my home. Our ver-dant for—est green, Ca-

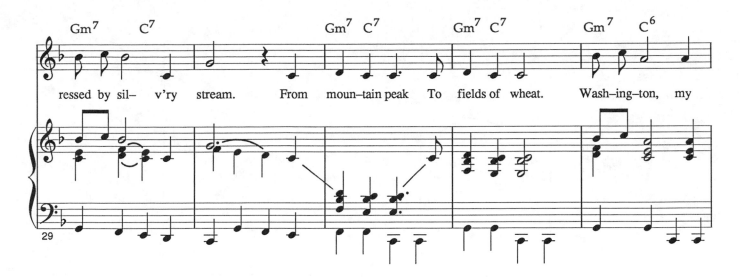

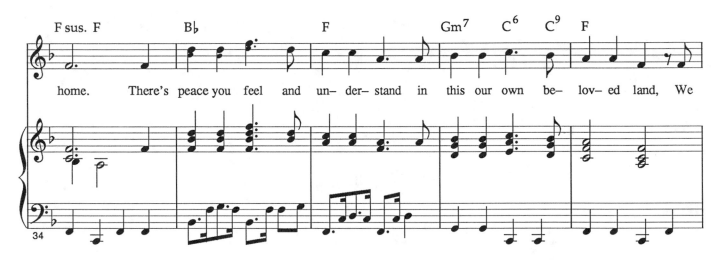

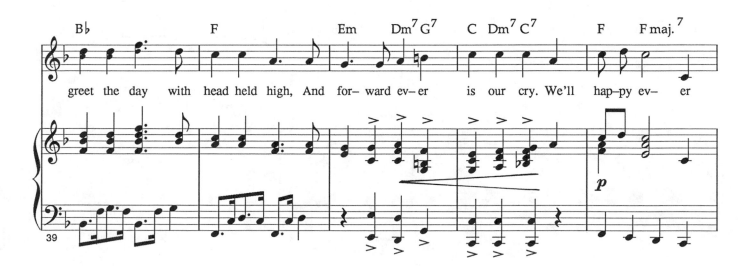

# It's A Hundred To One You're From Washington

Words and music by
Al Hoffman

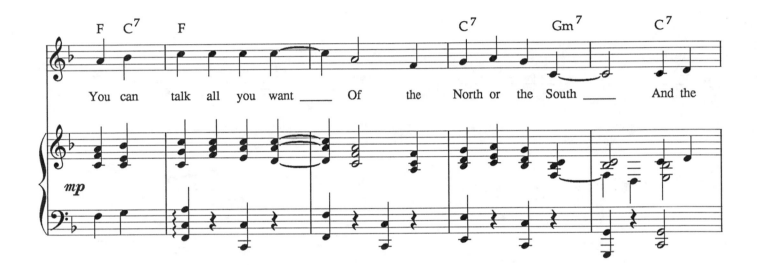

You can talk all you want ____ Of the North or the South ____ And the

glo–ries of the East or West, ____ But it's eas-y to tell ____ Where you're

141

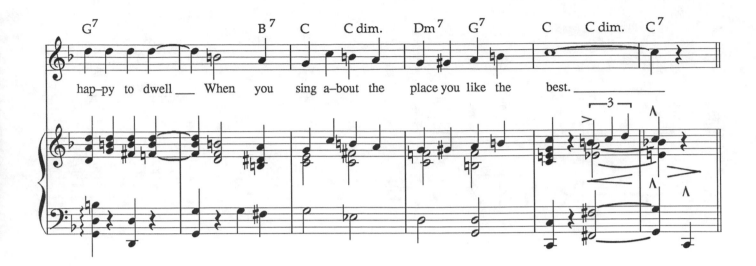

hap–py to dwell ___ When you sing a–bout the place you like the best. ___

**Chorus**

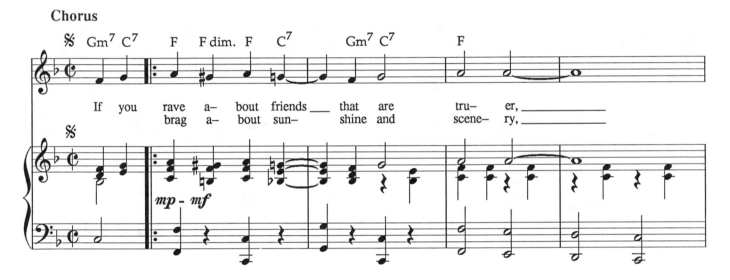

If you rave a– bout friends ___ that are tru– er, ___
brag a– bout sun– shine and scene– ry, ___

Boast a– bout skies ___ that are blu– er, ___ IT'S A HUN-DRED TO ONE
Beau– ti– ful flow– ers and green– 'ry, ___

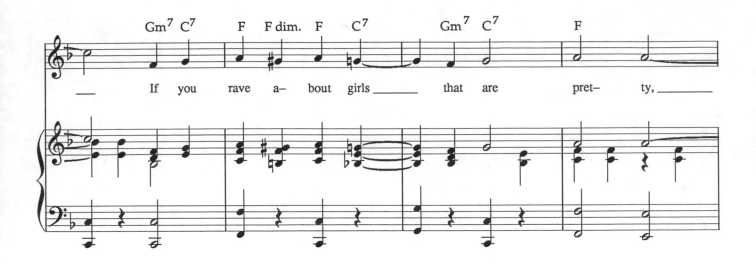

If you rave a- bout girls ___ that are pret― ty, ___

That are part of your heart ___ and your ci― ty, ___

___ IT'S A HUN-DRED TO ONE ___ YOU'RE FROM WASH― ING―TON, ___ A

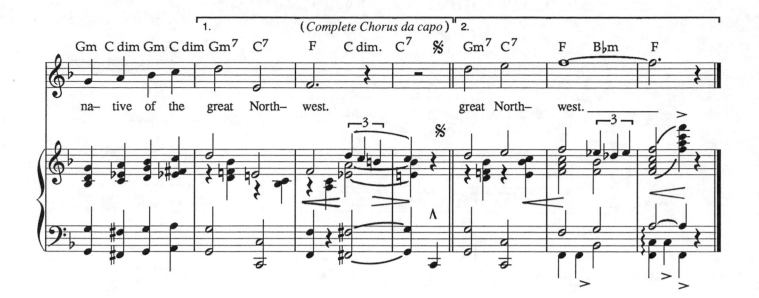

na– tive of the great North– west. great North– west.

# Our State Of Washington

Words and music by
Thomas "Red" Kelly

The crown of the na—tion A- bove all the rest, Pride of the

peo—ple who re— side in the West, A voice for the fu— ture where

each has a part, Our state of Wash—ing—ton, A state of the heart. The

moun– tains march migh–ti– ly to the o– cean's proud band, And

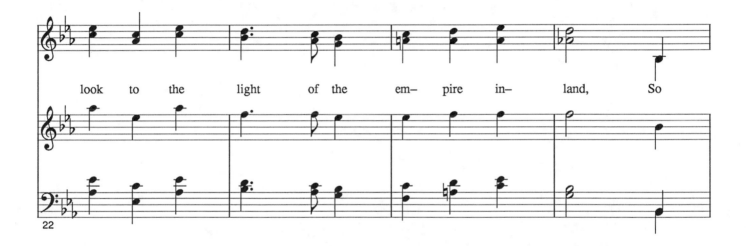

look to the light of the em– pire in– land, So

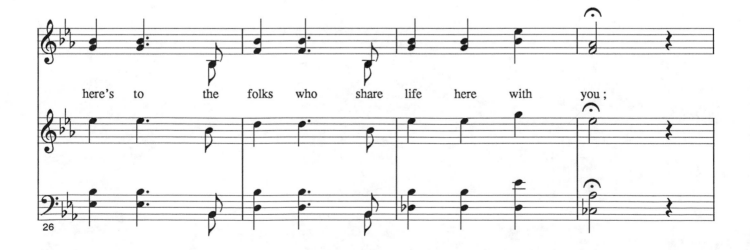

here's to the folks who share life here with you ;

Our state of Wash–ing–ton, It's love you we do.

*Rit.* _ _ _ *Rall.* _____

# Roll On, Columbia

Words by Woodie Guthrie
Music based on "Goodnight Irene"
by Huddie Ledbetter and John Lomax

149

25 pow— er is turn— ing our dark— ness to dawn, (so)

29 roll on, Co— lum— bia, roll on! _____

3. Tom Jefferson's vision would not let him rest,
   An empire he saw in the Pacific Northwest.
   Sent Lewis and Clark and they did the rest,
   Roll on, Columbia, roll on.

   *CHORUS*

4. It's there on your banks that we fought many a
         fight,
   Sheridan's boys in the blockhouse that night,
   They saw us in death but never in flight,
   Roll on, Columbia, roll on.

   *CHORUS*

5. At Bonneville now there are ships in the locks,
   The waters have risen and cleared all the rocks,
   Shiploads of plenty will steam past the docks,
   So roll on, Columbia, roll on.

*CHORUS*

6. And on up the river is Grand Coulee Dam,
   The mightiest thing ever built by a man,
   To run the great factories and water the land,
   It's roll on, Columbia, roll on.

*CHORUS*

7. These mighty men labored by day and by night,
   Matching their strength 'gainst the river's wild
         flight,
   Through rapids and falls they won the hard fight,
   Roll on, Columbia, roll on.

*CHORUS*

# Booster Songs

Many songs composed in the late 1800s and early 1900s were booster songs—written to attract settlers and new businesses to Washington towns. At the turn of the century, rivalry between western Washington towns was fierce as each town struggled to increase its population and industries. According to the *Journal of Events in Snohomish County History*, "while the rivalry was often in earnest, it was also a source of recreation and lively good fellowship for local 'boosters'— businessmen whose fervent partisanship sometimes approached fanaticism."

For unabashed boosterism few songs could surpass **"Go Way Back And Sit Down."** The lyrics for the song were written by the Everett Chamber of Commerce and first sung on February 5, 1902, to celebrate the tenth anniversary of the filing of the Everett Land Company's Plat of Everett. Everett's version of "Go Way Back And Sit Down" was a parody of a popular song of the same title written around 1880 by Al Johns. The popular inference from the phrase was that the subject seat himself on the nearest public convenience! We've included just a few verses for your enjoyment.

Walla Walla has been the subject of many songs; people just seem to like the way the name rolls off their tongues. **"Walla Walla Is My Home Town"** is a Northwest favorite. It was written by Eleanor Fletcher and was recorded by Joe Denney. Joe was a semi-pro ball player who can still be heard singing the national anthem in Seattle's Kingdome.

**"You'll Like Tacoma,"** a song written in 1909 by S. A. Huntington, Jr., was dedicated "To Tacoma and my Booster friend, Mr. Edward P. Kemmer." On the cover of the sheet music is an early picture of Tacoma with Mount Rainier in the background, and these words below: "The Spot for the Largest City west of The 'Great Divide.'" The song appears to have been written for the Alaska-Yukon-Pacific Exposition of 1909, perhaps to lure some prospective settlers away from Seattle, Tacoma's arch rival.

Tacoma has recently adopted a new slogan and a new song called "Tacoma: Full Of Nice Surprises." But another Tacoma song submitted for inclusion in this songbook contains lines the chamber of commerce is not likely to use. "The Aroma Of Tacoma" was written by Jim Torrence and Don Lemon. The first verse is as follows:

> The aroma of Tacoma takes your breath
> away
> You can tell it, you can smell it
> when you're fourteen miles away
> From the great Olympic Mountains,
> to the tide flats on the shore
> That aroma will be with us for now and
> evermore.

*Tacoma Lodge Band. Courtesy of Tacoma Historic Preservation Office.*

*At the 1914 Spokane Interstate Fair. Courtesy of Eastern Washington State Historical Society.*

**"My Home's In Cathlamet"** is Cleave Hedman's unique and delightful contribution to this chapter of hometown booster songs. He was a little concerned about including the fifth verse of "My Home's In Cathlamet," which is a bit derogatory to neighboring Naselle. So, to give Naselle its own chance to brag, Max Wilson, the "Bard of the Beach," wrote "Naselle Valley." Here's a chorus from that song:

> It's a grand place, this Naselle Valley
> Where the cool, clean zephyrs play
> Where there is a kindly greeting
> From the folks along the way.
> So it's goodbye Albuquerque
> Farewell Bering Sea
> It's the ideal place, the Naselle Valley
> For a wand'rer like me.
> —*"Naselle Valley"*
> *Sung to the tune of "It's A Long Way
> To Tipperary"*

Of the many songs contributed about Spokane none matched the bounce and vitality of **"Song Of Sunny Spokane,"** written by S. Luther Essick. "Song Of Sunny Spokane" was a family project—Essick wrote the words and his wife, Frances, wrote the musical arrangement. Their daughter, Joyce, graces the cover of the original sheet music. In a 1948 news article, Mr. Essick had this to say about the song:

> *This song comes from my heart in
> genuine appreciation of Spokane. . . it*

*was written because we have such a wonderful city. The purpose of it is to arouse some strong civic spirit for Spokane and to encourage others to write songs about our city.*

*The* essential ingredient for keeping the "wet side" of Washington green is a high concentration of Liquid Sunshine. That fact has provided inspiration to many Washington songwriters. Residents of western Washington live a schizophrenic existence, alternately cursing and blessing the gray clouds and ever-present moisture of the wet side of the mountains.

> Oh, give me a home where the skies are
> gray,
> Where the rain festival lasts from
> September to May
> Where I need my boots and my
> Bumbershoot,
> The elements better to battle;
> I love a soggy and foggy day,
> A typic'ly mis'rably drizzly day.
> The kind of a day that keeps tourists away;
> Oh give me a home in Seattle.
> It doesn't take long to adjust;
> We don't sprinkle to keep down the dust;
> The lawns all stay green, and the air
> washes clean
> And the natives don't tan, they just rust!
> —*From "Give Me A Home In Seattle"*
> *By Vivian Williams*

In her song **"Grey Skies,"** Mary Litchfield Tuel of Vashon Island captures the best of what rain can be, along with a look at island life: "Grey skies are just another expression of heaven. . . ."

In the early days of Richland's role as the site of the Hanford nuclear reservation, townspeople celebrated each summer with "Atomic Frontier Days." At one of these events, Jack Quinn, who worked at a local radio station, introduced **"It's A Good Town,"** written by Eleanor Fletcher. Eleanor, a prolific songwriter, was assisted by pianist Dorothy Brunton, who wrote down a song as Eleanor hummed or sang it. Mrs. Fletcher's songs included one called "I'd Like A Little Snow For Christmas," which was sent to a publisher just as "White Christmas" came along. The publisher suggested the Fletcher song would be of interest "when the novelty of this new number wears off."

Many songs celebrating "blossom times" in various cities were submitted for inclusion in this songbook. Frances Hare of the Yakima Valley Museum remembered **"When It's Blossom Time In Yakima Valley"** from the early 1940s. The song was written in 1938 by Jack Lawrence and was arranged by Harrison Miller, an organist at the Liberty Theatre.

Carlton Fitchett, prolific rhymester for the *Seattle Post-Intelligencer,* wrote a song called **"Puget Sound"** that struck a responsive chord in many Puget Sounders. The song first appeared in the *Post-Intelligencer* on December 1, 1944.

The song **"Godzilla Ate Tukwila,"** written and recorded in the 1970s by Dave Phillips of Seattle, highlights many Washington cities and towns that otherwise might not have been mentioned in this songbook. Then again, after hearing "Godzilla Ate Tukwila," maybe the towns would have preferred anonymity!

By far the largest number of songs submitted by the public for possible inclusion in *Washington Songs and Lore* were songs that embody the beauty and uniqueness of a specific town or region. These songs profile Washington at its best, through the vision of people who love it, and help to identify those characteristics that keep Washingtonians as firmly rooted here as the pine or the fir tree.

An Apple Red,
The State Flower too,
A North Yakima scene—
With greetings to you.

STREET SCENE NORTH YAKIMA

*"North Yakima" in 1909. Courtesy of Fort George Wright Museum Collection, Eastern Washington State Historical Society.*

# Go Way Back And Sit Down

Music by Al Johns
Words by the Everett
Chamber of Commerce, 1902

sev—eral towns on Pu—get Sound, a— long in 'Nine—ty— one, That

thought this spit a place not fit to____ build a town u— pon. A

change has come, hard work has won, and they've had to change their maps, The

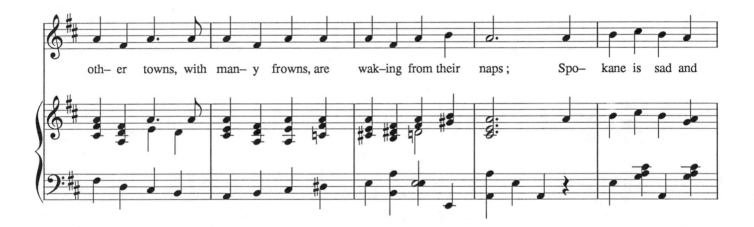

oth— er towns, with man— y frowns, are wak—ing from their naps; Spo— kane is sad and

Port—land's mad, and Ta-co— ma's in a sweat; —— What—com cries and Se— at— tle tries to

head off E— ver— ett. But we're here to stay and some near day we'll sure—ly lead the

bunch, We'll give Se—at—tle a case of rat— tle, and she must take this hunch :

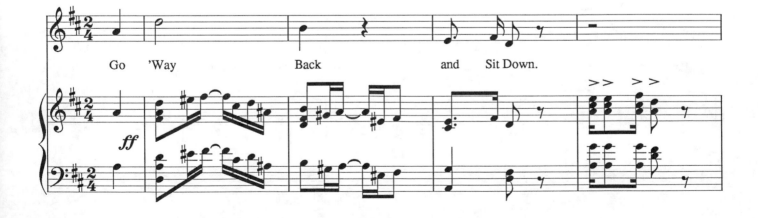

Go 'Way Back and Sit Down.

Boom–ers in your class are ea– sy found; You're

short on mon–ey but long on shout; You make a great bluff but ne–ver win out, Go

'Way Back and Sit Down!

2. For the county seat we did compete and won it out
   and out.
   Snohomish swore and rave and tore, and Ferg was
   put to rout.
   Nichols and Brownwell they worked like—well,
   they worked with might and main;
   They hired the boats, purchased the votes, and
   came through without a stain!
   Old Hank Hewitt saw us do it, and pledged his
   faith anew;
   "I'll build a mill, by the brick on the hill and
   finish the old thing too."
   But alas and alack! his faith grew slack, and pity
   but 'tis true—
   His start was bold but his feet got cold, so there's
   nothing for him to do but

*SECOND CHORUS*

*Go 'Way Back and Sit Down.*
*Things are moving in this here town.*
*Hank gave us the shake, but he'll see we're awake—*
*We could lose a few more and still take the cake—*
*Go 'Way Back and Sit Down!*

3. We've grown in fame but just the same, we'll not
   forget 'tis due
   To the pioneers who in early years blazed Hewitt
   Avenue.
   The names of these men like William Penn will be
   known in years to come
   As the ones who were true when things looked
   blue and the town was on the bum.
   To J. J. Clark all had to hark when his voice rose
   in acclaim—
   "Stand by the place, don't quit the race, we'll put
   New York to shame."
   First in the fight were Rucker and White and
   Swalwell and Jim Bell too,
   Mulford and Mills, Doc Cox with his pills, and
   many others as true—

*THIRD CHORUS*

*Come up front and sit down.*
*A new man in your class has just been found;*
*McChesney's got the stuff, for improvements he'll*
   *duff;*
*He never fails to dig, for we give him proper guff—*
*Come up front and sit down!*

4. When the sun goes down on the hot air town on
   the shores of Elliott Bay
   There's a great big hustle and a terrible bustle and
   the mayor begins to pray.
   He sends a message to the harbor board: "Grant
   our canal, we pray."
   An answer came quick that made Humes sick, for
   the board to him did say:

*FOURTH CHORUS*

*Go 'Way Back and Sit Down.*
*Everett's the only town on Puget Sound.*
*You are a back number, you haven't got the price,*
*Get back in your place, your petition's on ice—*
*Go 'Way Back and Sit Down!*

# Walla Walla Is My Home Town

Words and music by
Eleanor Fletcher

159

liked it so they named it twice, yes Wal-la Wal-la's my home town. _____ Gee, I'm town. ____

*A view of Walla Walla's main street, early 1920s.*
*Photograph by Wesley Andrews courtesy of Oregon Historical Society.*

# You'll Like Tacoma

Words and music by
S. A. Huntington, Jr.

**Marcia**

1. Way out West in Wash–ing–ton, Down on Pu– get

Sound _____ There's a port the best on earth, That's

known the world a— round _____ Five big rail— roads at its

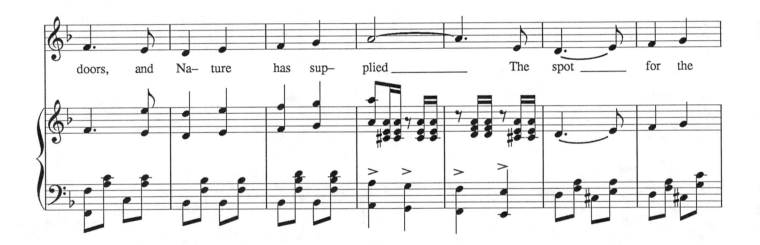

doors, and Na— ture has sup— plied _____ The spot _____ for the

larg— est Cit— y, West of the Great Di— vide _____

**Chorus**

You'll like Ta— co— ma, Where rail meets sail, Where all are prosp'—rous, hear—ty and

hale _____ Down on Com— mence—ment Bay, A "New York's" grow—ing

day by day. ___ Ta— co— ma, the peer of all. _____

2.    Everyone that comes out West, to see the A-Y-P
      Will not go back when once they see The City of
            Destiny.
      They will see like all the rest that it's the only
            place
      That has all the advantages to set all the world a
            pace.

      *CHORUS*

3.    Tacoma has the finest clime of all the U.S.A.
      And none die but the dead ones, down on
            Commencement Bay.
      Her women are the prettiest, her men are strong
            and true;
      Let me tell you stranger, Tacoma's the place for
            you.

      *CHORUS*

*Courtesy Washington State Historical Society.*

# My Home's In Cathlamet

Words and music by
Cleave Hedman

1. My home's in Cath— la— met where wea— ther is damp, It's the
2. Our log— gers now gai— ly do prom— e— nade dai— ly, Deep

moist to be say— ing the ver— y of least, With
in— to the for— ests of tim— ber so tall, There is

nine hun— dred in— ches of rain— fall per year, We have
fir and there's cot— ton— wood, some I've for— got— ten would

166

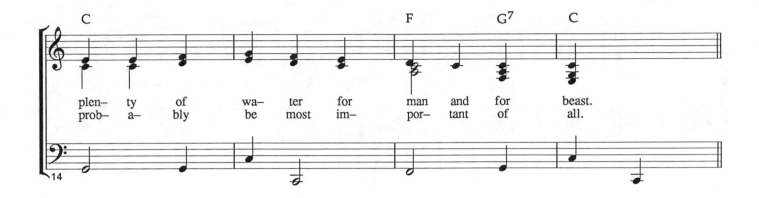

plen—ty of wa—ter for man and for beast.
prob—a—bly be most im—por—tant of all.

2. For Flora and Fauna, they promenade at dawn
It's no wonder they're tired, a schedule so mean
With axes a-swingin' and chain saws a-ringin'
Such tender devotion you never have seen.

3. When workday is over, they go home to muvver
Who fixes her babies great mountains of food
There is one herd of cattle for each hungry logger,
And tons of potatoes so creamy and good.

4. When the Lord made Cathlamet, it filled Him
with pleasure
And He quickly went on to a place called Naselle
The name of the former He chose to call Heaven
The name of the latter I'd rather not tell.

5. Oh come to Cathlamet and see the great river
Oh come see the forest so verdant and green
Observe the wild loggers way up in the tree tops
The stranger of creatures you never have seen.

# Song Of Sunny Spokane

Words and music by
S. Luther Essick
Arr. by Frances Reed Essick

You've heard of the turn–ing wag–on wheels, A–roll–ing a–roll–ing a–long, And I foll–owed the trail of the wa–gon wheels, And now I can sing this song.

Skies are blue and friend–ships true, In sun– ny old Spo–kane. Moth–ers croon a mel–low tune, In sun–ny old Spo–kane. Your life's a lit– tle bright–er, The load a lit– tle light–er,

The snow a lit–tle whit–er, In sun–ny old Spo–kane. The li–lacs bloom 'neath a sil–ver moon, In

sun–ny old Spo–kane. Stay a while and learn to smile, In a friend–ly hap–py land. You'll

learn to laugh and learn to play, In the good home fash–ioned Spo–kane way. If you try it out

you'll ne–ver stray, From sun–ny old Spo–kane.

# Grey Skies

Music and words by
Mary Litchfield Tuel

**1st Chorus**

Grey skies are just a—noth—er ex— press—ion of hea— ven,

Rain clouds don't slow me down as thru' this world I roam,

Look-in' down the road at the end of the rain, I can see a rain— bow, At the

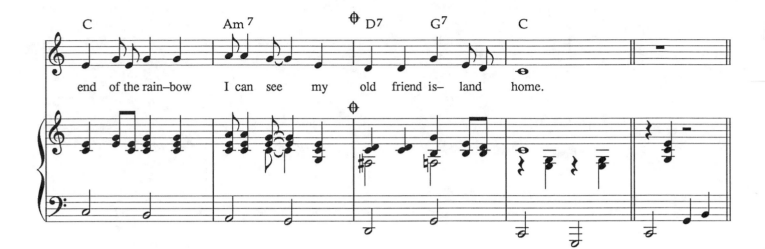

end of the rain—bow I can see my old friend is— land home.

**2nd Chorus**

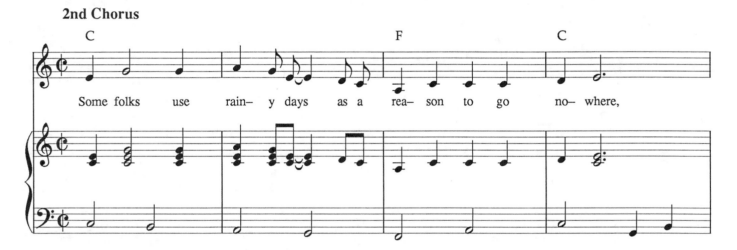

Some folks use rain— y days as a rea— son to go no— where,

Some folks may— be ain't go—ing no— where an—y way,

My folks they chop their wood and sit a–round the fire,

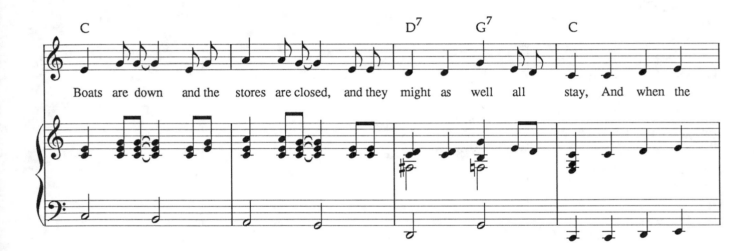

Boats are down and the stores are closed, and they might as well all stay, And when the

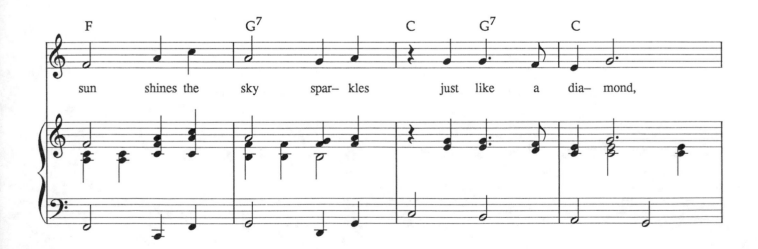

sun shines the sky spar–kles just like a dia–mond,

Blue fire and ro— sy gold go danc— in' on the waves, And when the

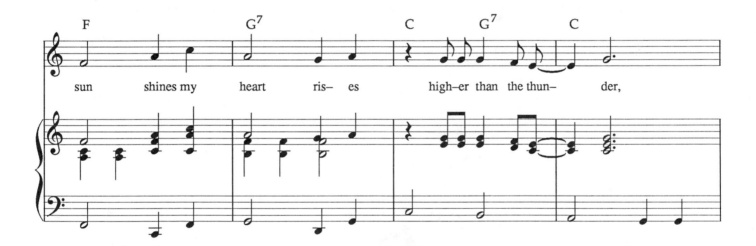

sun shines my heart ris— es high—er than the thun— der,

Light my way thru' ev— ry com— ing dark and rain—y day. _____

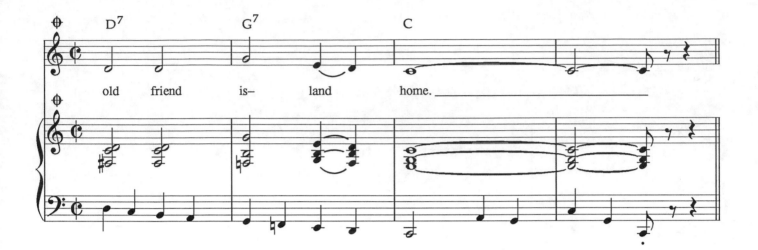

old  friend  is-  land  home._____

# It's A Good Town

Words and music by
Eleanor Fletcher

1. If you're look-ing for a darn good
2. It was born in nine-teen for- ty

town,_____ Looked a lot of plac- es up and turned them down, _____ Just
three,_____ And a fin- er place you'll nev- er, nev- er see, _____ We

take a look at Rich–land, so fine in ev–'ry way, It's the most ex-cit- ing vil- lage in the
all pitched in and built it, And real–ly built it right, Be— tween Mon–day morn-ing and a

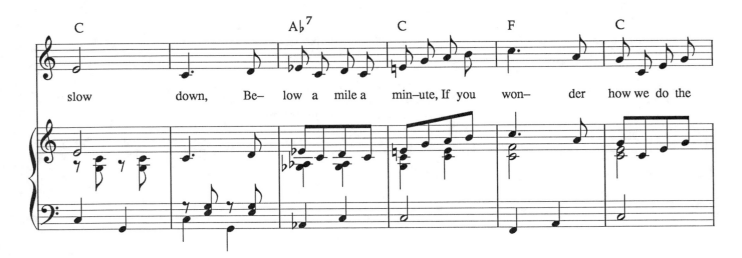

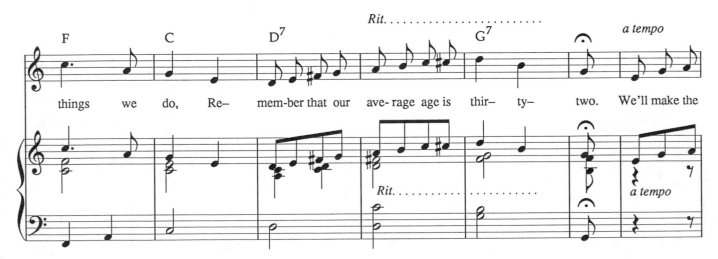

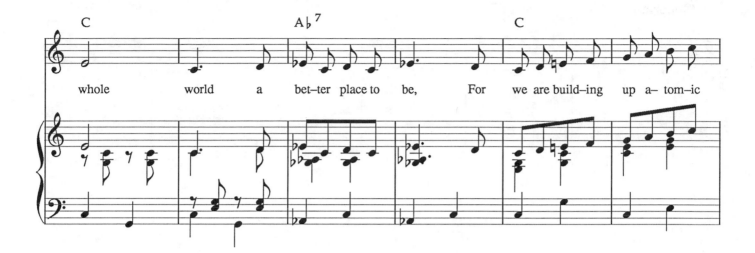

whole world a bet–ter place to be, For we are build–ing up a–tom–ic

en–er–gy. And when folks see Rich–land you will hear them say, It's the

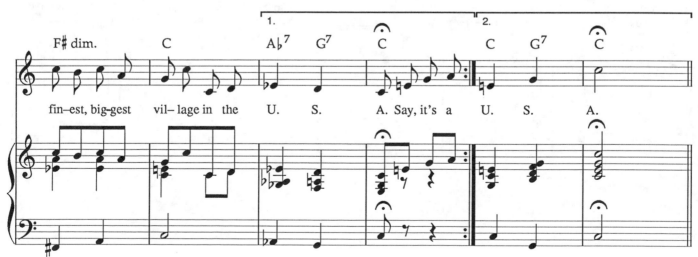

fin–est, big–gest vil–lage in the U. S. A. Say, it's a U. S. A.

# When It's Blossom Time In Yakima Valley

Words and music by
Jack Lawrence

Moderato

1. I'm so wear— y to— night and I long for the sight, Of a
2. Let me wan— der a— gain where the whis— per— ing wind thru the

val— ley a— way in the west, _____ Where the fra— grant per— fume of the
trees plays a sweet mel— o— dy, _____ 'Neath the moon— light's ca— ress there I'll

or– chards in bloom, Casts a spell that no words can ex– press. _____
find hap– pi– ness, With a mai– den who's wait– ing for me. _____

**Chorus**

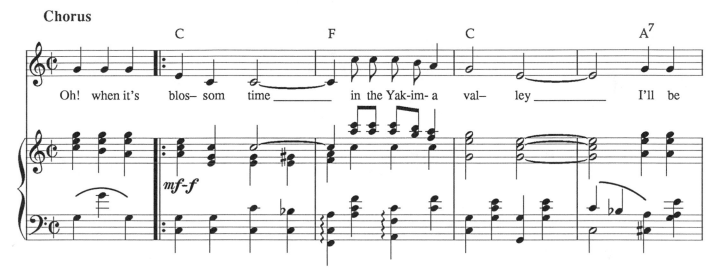

Oh! when it's blos– som time _____ in the Yak–im– a val– ley _____ I'll be

drift– ing back to– ward that par– a– dise, _____ I left this heart o' mine _____

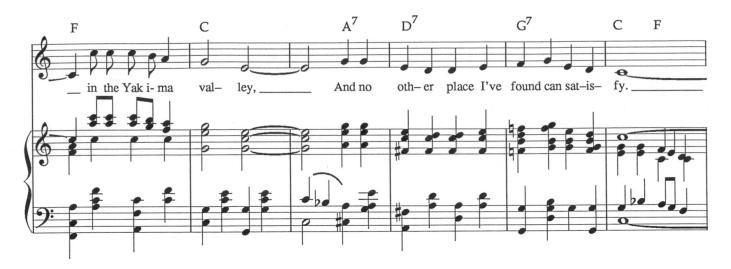

in the Yak i- ma val– ley, _____ And no oth–er place I've found can sat–is– fy. _____

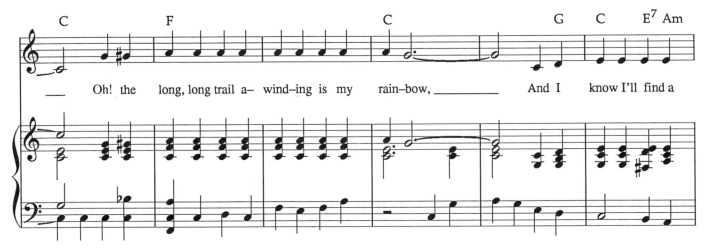

Oh! the long, long trail a– wind–ing is my rain–bow, _____ And I know I'll find a

treas–ure at the end, _____ Oh! when it's blos–som time _____ in the Yak-im- a

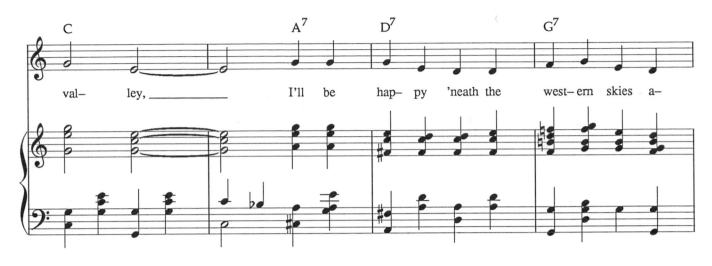

val- ley, _____ I'll be hap- py 'neath the west-ern skies a-

1.
gain. _____ Oh! when it's

2.
gain. _____

The cover of this promotional brochure
depicts landscape typical of the Yakima
Valley fruit-growing region, of
which Wenatchee is a part.
Courtesy of Washington State
Historical Society.

# Puget Sound

**Andantino expressivo**

Words and music by
Carlton Fitchett

1. As hap–py as a but–ter clam when tides are high I sing, A grate–ful ode to Pu–get Sound, the land of eve–ry–thing, I love it from Tu–la–lip to Puy–all–up, Sequim and Pysht, And to the Do–se–wal–lips where

man- y times I've fished. From Brin–non to the Bo– ga–chiel, From Lum–mi to La Push, And

from the lord–ly Sol Duc to love–ly Duck–a– bush, From Sam–ish to Sam–mam–ish, Su–

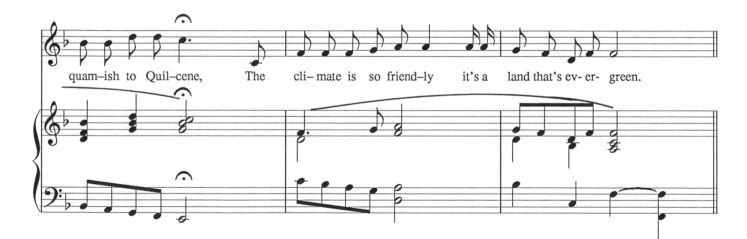

quam–ish to Quil–cene, The cli–mate is so friend–ly it's a land that's ev– er– green.

2.   There's peace on the Skykomish
     On the Queets and on the Hoh,
     There's calm on the Nisqually
     Born of ageless ice and snow;
     A land that Nature loves so much
     She stays the whole year 'round
     I'd trade a royal palace
     For a shack on Puget Sound!

*SECOND CHORUS*

*There's Chimacum and Steilacoom*
*Where spouts the geoduck;*
*The singing Stillaguamish*
*And the swirling Skookumchuck*
*And Moclips and Copalis*
*Where the razor clams abound—*
*—A little bit of heaven*
*Is a shack on Puget Sound.*

# Godzilla Ate Tukwila

Words and music by
Dave Phillips

2. Now some folks saw him hurryin' down the south
     side of Burien
   And they all yelled out, "Oh, no!"
   He wandered into Sea-Tac, and he ordered
       himself a Big Mac,
   Then said, "Better make that an Ellensburger, to
       go."

3. Of course, he took a big bite of Bothell and says,
       "Uh, that tastes awful,"
   Then he went and ate North Enumclaw.
   He drank up Lake Chelan, then he piddled on
       Spokane,
   And fertilized half of Yakima.

4. It was a real pity, what he did at Tri-Cities.
   People from Walla Walla got scared, too.
   Down at Longacres, I saw him comin', ten to one,
       I started runnin',
   Why, I even ran right by Seattle Slew.

5. Now he chewed up Wenatchee, and that made his
       throat scratchy.
   People from North Bend said, "Golly, that's
       scary."
   He marched clear 'round the edge of Puget Sound
   And sank the Mukilteo Ferry.

6. He ate up Bellingham, he left Mt. Vernon burnin',
   He was workin' his way on down south
   And I told him, "Don't put Lynnwood in your
       tummy, you overgrown dummy.
   That place'll stick to the roof of your mouth."

7. I guess you know he ate up Tonasket, put Omak
       in a basket
   And he marched on back across Cascade Ridge.
   He says, "I think I'll just ramble up there to Point
       Gamble
   Then I can sink half the Hood Canal Bridge."

8. You know, they found Godzilla asleep out here on
       the golf course
   And they called out the Army, the Navy, and the
       Air Force.
   They says, "Well, we'll zap his backside with
       plutonium and uranium."
   That made him mad, and he ate the Dome
       Stadium.

9. He chewed up Chehalis, and Kelso, and Centralia.
   Auburn and Kent were on his route.
   He ate up Bellevue, and Kirkland, and Monroe.
   He tasted Everett, and he spit it out.

10. Yeah, I saw Godzilla eat up Tukwila,
    This time he tried Ballard for dessert.
    And I could hear him say as he wandered out of
        sight,
    "Hiccup! Urp! Hey, Dixie, this state's all right!"

# Index

*Page numbers in italics refer to musical scores.*